D0059057

ARCTIC EXPLORERS

In Search of the Northwest Passage

FRANCES HERN

VICTORIA · VANCOUVER · CALGARY

Heritage House Publishing Company Ltd.
#108 – 17665 66A Avenue
Surrey, BC V3S 2A7
www.heritagehouse.ca

Heritage House Publishing Company Ltd.
PO Box 468
Custer, WA
98240-0468

Library and Archives Canada Cataloguing in Publication
Hern, Frances
    Arctic explorers: in search of the Northwest Passage / Frances Hern.

Includes bibliographical references.
ISBN 978-1-926613-29-1

    1. Explorers—Canada, Northern—Biography. 2. Northwest Passage—Discovery and exploration. 3. Arctic regions—Discovery and exploration. 4. Canada, Northern—Discovery and exploration. I. Title

G634.H47 2010   917.1904   C2009-906901-6

Series editor: Lesley Reynolds.
Cover design: Chyla Cardinal. Interior design: Frances Hunter.
Cover photo: HMS *Alert* and *Discovery* on the Arctic expedition of 1865–66 by William Frederick Mitchell, Fine Art Photographic Library/CORBIS (AALQ001794).

 Mixed Sources
Cert no. SW-COC-001271
© 1996 FSC
FSC   The interior of this book was printed on 100% post-consumer recycled paper, processed chlorine free and printed with vegetable-based inks.

Heritage House acknowledges the financial support for its publishing program from the Government of Canada through the Canada Book Fund (CBF), Canada Council for the Arts and the province of British Columbia through the British Columbia Arts Council and the Book Publishing Tax Credit.

 BRITISH COLUMBIA
ARTS COUNCIL
Supported by the Province of British Columbia

 Canada Council   Conseil des Arts
for the Arts   du Canada

13 12 11 10   1 2 3 4 5
Printed in Canada

To my parents, Win and Ron,
who shared with me their love of a good story

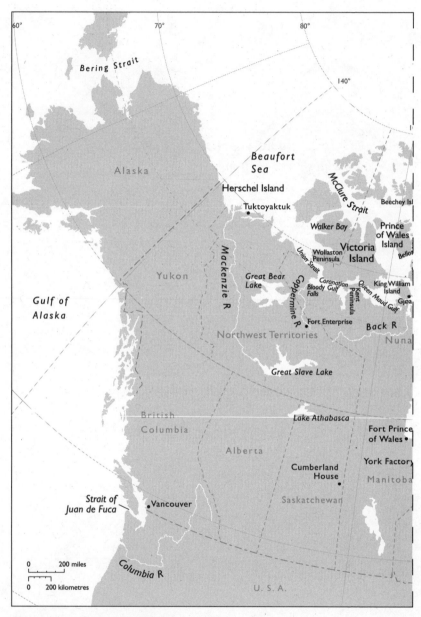

Northern Canada and the Northwest Passage

MAP COURTESY OF TOUCHWOOD EDITIONS

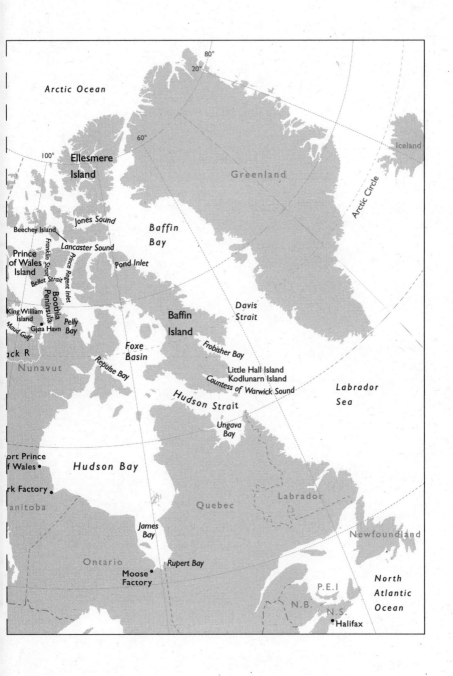

Contents

Author's Note

Although metric measurement was adopted in Canada in 1971, the nautical mile is still used at sea. To ensure consistency, accuracy and to avoid confusion, the author has decided to use imperial measurements throughout this book.

Prologue

SIR HUGH WILLOUGHBY WAS WAITING *aboard the* Bona Esperanza *for the pilot to guide his flotilla of three ships into the harbour at Vardø, on the northeastern tip of Norway, when a storm hit. Gale-force gusts channelled down the cliffs and battered the ships. Afraid they would be smashed against the rocks, Willoughby gave the order to run back out to sea where his men struggled to furl the sails so the wind wouldn't tear them to shreds. The sailors spent an anxious night adrift on an ocean gone wild, where icy mist obscured any warning of approaching shoals or icebergs.*

It was August 1553, and Willoughby had been commissioned to find a shorter and safer route from England to Cathay (now China). He was immensely relieved when the storm blew itself out in the early hours of the morning. By daybreak, the mist had dispersed, but that wasn't the only thing gone—there was no sign of the Edward Bonaventure. They were now without their chief navigator. Willoughby's men tried to sail the Bona Esperanza and the Bona Confidentia back to Vardø, but they couldn't find it. They couldn't find any land at all.

They sailed across the Barents Sea for seven weeks, hopelessly lost, and finally anchored in a desolate but sheltered nook in the mouth of a river. September was almost gone, and daylight hours were fast diminishing. Ice began to coat the two ships and form on the water around them. They had little choice but to stay there until spring.

Russian fishermen found the ships the following summer. The English sailors were all dead, but strangely, they showed no signs of discomfort from scurvy, starvation or freezing, which were the most likely causes of death. Sir Hugh Willoughby was seated at his desk, his logbook before him, pen in hand. Other men had died while they were eating, spoons still in their mouths. One man had been opening a locker. Even the dogs looked as though they had died instantly and without warning.

The fishermen stared at the disturbing scene and wondered what unspeakable event had caused the deaths of these unfortunate men.

1

Martin Frobisher
(ca. 1536–1594)

MARTIN FROBISHER WAS A SURVIVOR. His parents died when he was young, and he was packed off from Yorkshire to live in London with an uncle. He didn't like math, and his handwriting was hardly legible, but he showed no fear of the unknown and had a knack for getting on with life. When he was about 17, his uncle signed him up as an apprentice merchant with a business associate's company.

Frobisher sailed for West Africa in a flotilla of three ships in August 1553. While in Guinea, waiting for a cargo of peppers to be harvested and loaded, the English sailors were plagued by mosquitoes and suffocating heat. Some of them developed a high fever with vomiting and collapsed from extreme exhaustion. The captain abandoned his cargo and set sail for England, but his men began to die from the dehydrating fever that turned their vomit black and their skin yellow. Yellow fever killed all but 40 of the 140 men aboard, including the captain and pilots. The survivors sailed home using a combination of skill, luck and sheer willpower. Frobisher was among them.

Despite this traumatic experience, he returned to the Gold Coast of West Africa the following year with another small flotilla. As one of the least experienced men on board, and therefore the most expendable, he was taken ashore as a hostage to show the captain's honest intentions. Before trade negotiations even began, a Portuguese ship appeared and, to protect Portugal's monopoly on trade, opened fire on the flotilla. The captain sailed away, and the governor handed Frobisher over to the Portuguese. When the ships returned to England, short one apprentice merchant, no one expected to see Frobisher again. However, the resourceful young man eventually escaped and was able to work his way home.

By the time Frobisher returned to England, Queen Mary had died and her half-sister had been crowned Elizabeth I. Mary's husband, King Philip II of Spain, had exhausted England's resources for the benefit of his own country, and Queen Elizabeth's treasury was empty. The Catholic Queen Mary had been busy ridding the country of Protestant heretics by burning them at the stake. As a result, many English were happy to have the Protestant Elizabeth on the throne. However, the position of monarch was precarious, and the newly installed queen did not want to risk her popularity by taxing her subjects. Even so, she was well aware of the vulnerability of her bankrupt island and knew that she needed money to strengthen the navy that her father, King Henry VIII, had begun to build.

By this time, Frobisher was a tall and imposing young man with an intimidating temper. He was full of energy and enthusiasm, accustomed to the hardships of life at sea and had gained valuable shipboard experience during his hazardous voyages. Frobisher was also willing to bend the letter of the law if there was money to be made. He became a privateer or, more accurately, a pirate.

The line between privateering and piracy was a fine one. A privateer had the British Admiralty's permission to seize and plunder enemy ships. Those belonging to allies were to be left alone, but Frobisher's definition of an enemy ship seems to have been any unescorted foreign ship, sometimes Spanish, that lacked witnesses to report how it disappeared. Queen Elizabeth couldn't afford to antagonize King Philip, who would keep the French from invading England as long as he thought Elizabeth might marry him. She was obliged to charge Frobisher with piracy and have him thrown in jail on several occasions, releasing him when the hue and cry died down. No doubt some of the profit from sales of the cargo he seized found its way into Elizabeth's treasury to ensure her continued favour.

With Elizabeth's navy still in its infancy, the privateers

helped to assert England's interests at sea, but attacks became more frequent and more indiscriminate as the number of privateers rapidly grew. Their success began to undermine the delicate relationship between England and Spain, and Elizabeth was embarrassed into further action. She gave Frobisher command of a fleet of four ships and ordered him to intercept privateers and search for illicitly seized goods. While Frobisher had a reputation for looking after his own interests to the detriment of everyone else, he was not interested in exposing his fellow thieves. What he was interested in was finding a safer route to the riches of the East.

As seafaring nations began to build stronger, more reliable ships that were capable of longer voyages, sailors began to search for another route to the East. Adventurous men could make a great deal of money by sailing ships back to England laden with silks, gold and especially spices. The food in Europe and Britain was bland and boring. Cinnamon, nutmeg, pepper and cloves were worth their weight in silver, but the routes to reach them were hazardous.

The old overland routes east that formed the Silk Road, from Constantinople (now Istanbul) in Turkey to Chang'an (now Xi'an) in China, had fallen into disuse around 1400 after the Mongol empire crumbled. When the Muslim Ottomans conquered Christian Constantinople approximately 50 years later, it seemed unlikely that these routes would be revived.

Christopher Columbus tried sailing west from Spain and found Cuba, the Bahamas, Haiti and the Dominican Republic. John Cabot sailed west from England and found Newfoundland. The situation had grown more complicated by the beginning of Frobisher's century. The Catholic pope had sanctioned a Spanish monopoly on all trade and commerce in the Americas and a Portuguese monopoly in Africa. These two dominant maritime powers did all they could to protect their valuable monopolies. This meant that any ship that survived the treacherous waters and terrible storms of Cape Horn around the tip of South America, or the Cape of Good Hope around the southern tip of Africa, was likely to be attacked by the Spanish or the Portuguese (as Frobisher had discovered earlier on the Gold Coast). However, there was one direction yet to be explored—north.

Few men had sailed as far north as the Arctic, and even fewer had returned. Those who had travelled to the Arctic told tales of strange one-horned beasts, weeks of winter darkness, intense cold and treacherous ice. Nevertheless, there were courageous men filled with wanderlust and curiosity who hoped to make a name for themselves and, if they were particularly lucky, a fortune.

Martin Frobisher was such a man, but an Arctic voyage was expensive. Although he had married a widow with money, it wasn't nearly enough, and he soon drained his wife's resources. He approached the Muscovy Company, which had formed in 1553 to encourage exploration of a northeast passage. Initially, the investors turned him down. However, with the help of Michael Lok (the company's general manager in London), who knew the merchant business and understood the potential for trade with the Indies, the Muscovy Company directors were eventually persuaded to invest in the voyage.

Frobisher still didn't have enough money for a large ship, but he bought the *Michael* and had the *Gabriel* built. At about 30 tons and measuring 50 by 14 feet, the *Gabriel* was slightly larger than the *Michael*. To complete his flotilla, he built a small sailboat for exploring water too shallow for the *Gabriel* and the *Michael*. Frobisher had seen first-hand how inadequate food and serious illness could jeopardize the safety of an entire crew, so he put considerable thought into equipping and provisioning his ships. As well as the standard stores of salted beef and biscuits, he purchased enough oatmeal, rice, salt cod, cheese, bacon, dried peas, flour and butter to last 12 months, if carefully rationed. He also loaded beer, brandy, wine, oil and vinegar, and the best available maps and charts. A small library included books about previous voyages. For navigation he had geometric instruments, numerous hourglasses and compasses, an astrolabe, a cross-staff and a lead line. Martin Frobisher and Christopher Hall (the *Gabriel*'s pilot) put the weeks before they left to good use learning celestial navigation.

Sailing North at Last

The three ships finally sailed down the Thames River on
June 7, 1576. However, strong headwinds confined them to
the English coast for two weeks. By the time they reached
the Shetland Islands, north of Scotland's mainland, the
Michael had sprung a leak. They stopped to make repairs
and refill their water barrels. In early July, they battered
their way west across the North Atlantic through a series
of storms. On July 11, they sighted a coastline they mistook
for Frisland, an island shown on early charts that did not
exist. This was likely Greenland, and they kept clear of its
ice-clogged shores made treacherous by thick fog. They continued west across Davis Strait and ran into another storm.
The three ships lost contact and the small sailboat simply
disappeared, presumably swamped and sunk with her four-
man crew. The *Michael* sighted the coastline of Labrador,
but since the way ahead was choked with great sheets of ice,
her 12-man crew decided to turn around and sail home.
When they reached England, they reported that the northwest route to Cathay was impassable and that the sailboat
and the *Gabriel* were lost at sea with all hands.

The 18-man crew on the *Gabriel* would likely have sailed
for home, too, given the choice, but Frobisher did not give
up easily. When another storm hit, the worst so far, the
Gabriel was knocked onto her side. Icy water tore at her
rigging and poured down the hatches, flushing out some of
her cargo. Frobisher struggled along the slippery gunwale of

the heaving ship to adjust the foresail and yelled to his men to chop down the mizzenmast. With less sail to catch the gale-force winds, the ship righted a little. Seeing this, the panicking sailors wanted to chop down the mainmast, too. However, without enough sail to propel the *Gabriel* forward they would be condemned to drift with the currents. Frobisher managed to stop them and fired off orders to lower all but one small foresail, man the pumps and regain control of the ship. The storm gradually subsided, and the *Gabriel* limped westward while her crew made repairs to her rigging.

On August 10, Hall and four other men rowed in the *Gabriel*'s tender to a small island, which they later named Little Hall Island. Looking for souvenirs of their first foray ashore, Hall picked up a black rock from the beach. They also found a shallow bay where they could anchor and recaulk the *Gabriel*'s hull.

As they continued to sail west, Frobisher grew convinced that he had found the passage to Cathay. He thought that the coastline off his port (left) side was America, while that off his starboard (right) side was Asia. He was, in fact, sailing down Frobisher Bay, which he named Frobishers Streytes. As the straits began to narrow and fill with small islands, he stopped to reconnoitre. Several men, including Hall, clambered up a hill on one of the islands with Frobisher, hoping to see a clear passage leading west. Frobisher thought he saw one, but before they could have a good look, they were distracted by the sight of strangely dressed people paddling seven small boats toward them.

The English sailors had no way of knowing if these little people were friendly or hostile, so they ran back to their tender and quickly rowed out to the *Gabriel* to prepare for a possible attack. The strangers showed no sign of hostility, and Hall returned to shore to try to make friends. After much gesturing, he left one English sailor with the Inuit as a sign of goodwill and persuaded one of the strangers to board the *Gabriel*. The Inuk stared with great curiosity at this ship made almost entirely of wood, and with good reason. With the Arctic growing season of about 40 days, trees grew less than half an inch each year, making wood scarce and valuable.

Over the next few days, the English and the Inuit visited back and forth between the camp and the ship. The women wore blue streaks of dye down their cheeks and around their eyes. They all made expressions of distaste when they sampled the sailors' food. The sailors recalled stories of cannibals as they watched the Inuit chew on chunks of raw fish and seal meat. The sailors traded mirrors, bells and beads for polar bear and seal skins. Both groups tried to communicate but found it hard to understand each other. Frobisher asked about the straits. He thought the Inuit said that they opened up again two days' travel northwest from their current position, and he promised a male Inuk a knife if he would stay on board to guide the *Gabriel* through to the South Sea (the Pacific Ocean). The Inuit's only source of metal was from meteorites, and these were rare finds. They made tools from animal sinew and bone, so a metal knife was a much-coveted item. The Inuk appeared to agree to the deal, and Frobisher ordered five of his sailors to row the man back to camp so that he could tell his family and collect personal items for the journey.

Being cautious, Frobisher instructed his men to drop the Inuk guide within sight of the *Gabriel*. Ignoring his instructions, they rowed around the point out of sight of the ship. When they failed to return, Frobisher suspected that the Inuit had taken his men by force, perhaps because they wanted the ship's tender. Without it, Frobisher couldn't reach shore to see what was happening at the Inuit camp. For two days, he sailed the *Gabriel* up and down the coast as close to the shoreline as her draft would allow. He saw nothing. Frobisher ordered his men to fire the cannon and blast their trumpets, hoping to recall his missing men. There was no response.

Frobisher considered his options. It was possible that his five men had grown fed up with conditions on board the ship and had deserted. However, if they were being held against their will, he didn't want to sail off without them. He, of all men, knew what that felt like. Even worse was the fact that he couldn't continue to explore without his tender. He was still pacing and fuming a few days later when a group of Inuit paddled their kayaks out to the *Gabriel*.

Recognizing the man who had first come aboard, Frobisher had an idea. These strangers loved gifts. He offered the Inuk a large bell, and as the man paddled closer and reached for it, Frobisher leaned over and yanked him and his kayak out of the water. Now Frobisher had a hostage and could negotiate an exchange. There was just one problem. The man's companions didn't understand what Frobisher wanted. If they knew anything about the missing sailors, they made no sign, nor did they attempt to exchange prisoners.

While there were still a few days of August left, snow was beginning to fall. The *Gabriel* had no tender so, even if she found a suitable anchorage, her men could only reach shore by swimming through frigid water. Almost one-third of her crew were missing, maybe murdered for all Frobisher knew, leaving barely enough hands to sail the ship. Taking solace in the fact that he had an Inuk and his kayak to prove that they had indeed reached unknown lands, Frobisher gave orders to set sail for England.

When he reached London in early October, his investors were delighted to find that their ship had not been lost at sea after all. Frobisher was celebrated for his great achievement. His wife was less thrilled. Frobisher had made no provision for her or her children (from a previous marriage) while he was at sea, and she was now living in poverty. The Inuk and his kayak aroused much curiosity, but unfortunately the man had no immunity to foreign germs. He caught a cold and died soon after reaching England.

Despite any doubts Frobisher may have had about the navigability of his straits, he insisted that he had found a northwest passage to Cathay and worked hard to drum up support for another voyage. Queen Elizabeth was enthusiastic about him returning to this newly discovered land that she named Meta Incognita (Unknown Shore), but she was not willing to contribute any money unless the odds of making a profit were high. Frobisher's first voyage had gone over budget. Michael Lok, the Muscovy Company treasurer, had personally covered the loss and was still trying to balance the accounts. The investors would likely have voted against funding another voyage but for the piece of rock picked up by Hall on Little Hall Island.

The loaf-sized rock was the colour of sea coal. As it was the first thing they had found in the new land, Frobisher had given it to Lok as a memento. Lok was desperately looking for a way to replace the money he had invested in the voyage, so he broke off pieces of the black rock and gave them to different assayers. One of these assayers, a Venetian, showed Lok a small amount of gold that he said he'd recovered from Lok's sample. When Lok asked why the other assayers had told him their samples were worthless, the Venetian implied that it was because he had a better technique. Over the following months, Lok tried to think of a way to collect and profit from the ore without Frobisher's knowledge, but Frobisher and Hall were the only people who knew where the black rock had been found. Lok confided in Sir Francis Walsingham, Queen Elizabeth's secretary of state. Walsingham had heard get-rich-quick schemes like this one before and was skeptical at first. He eventually insisted that Frobisher be told about the gold and that a report be submitted to the queen.

Plans for a second voyage were laid out, and as rumours of gold began to circulate, gold fever took over. Eager new investors bought an interest in the voyage. Queen Elizabeth lent Frobisher the 200-ton *Ayde* for use as his flagship. While Frobisher was assured of another voyage, the primary goal was no longer exploration. He was told to transport miners to the deposits of black rock. Only when they were busy mining ore could Frobisher use the smaller ships to search for the five sailors who went missing on his first voyage and to explore farther west. If the assayers on the voyage tested rocks that were gold bearing, then Frobisher's orders were to strip his ships to make room for maximum loads of ore. If the rocks were worthless, he was to send the *Ayde* back to England before sailing the *Gabriel* and the *Michael* on to Cathay. He was also ordered to bring back "up to ten" healthy Inuit, without causing any ill feelings among the indigenous people. Frobisher may not have been entirely happy with these orders, but he didn't argue. Besides, if he brought back holds full of gold-bearing ore he would be a wealthy man.

Gold Fever
The ships sailed on May 31, 1577, and the navigators were

careful not to record any details that would pinpoint the specific location of the gold-bearing rocks. Without the storms that had plagued them the previous year, the sailors made good time and reached Little Hall Island by mid-July. Frobisher took a party of soldiers and gentlemen ashore to claim the new land for his queen. His soldiers piled stones into a cairn on the summit of a hill at the entrance to Frobishers Streytes. One of them sounded a trumpet and everyone kneeled. Frobisher named the hill Mount Warwick and gave thanks for their safe journey and the treasure they had found.

When Frobisher saw two unarmed Inuit onshore the next day, he was reminded of his instructions to take some of the local inhabitants back to England. He and Hall pretended they wanted to trade and seized the two men. The Inuit fought and broke free. They grabbed their bows from behind a rock and fired arrows as Hall and Frobisher ran back to their boat. An arrow pierced Frobisher's buttock, but one of his waiting men fired a gun and it was the Inuit's turn to run. A strong Cornish sailor wrestled one of them to the ground and held him captive. As this was taking place, a storm blew in. There was no way the sailors could manoeuvre their small boat through the great gusts and icy waves to the ships anchored out of sight in deeper water. Members of the shore party spent a miserable night lying on the hard, icy cliffs and keeping a keen lookout for their prisoner's angry friends. Sore from his arrow wound, Frobisher worried that the wind gusts would batter his ships against the ice. The storm died down overnight, and when his cold and hungry men rowed him out to the ships he was greatly relieved to find them still afloat.

Over the following weeks, the assayers tested outcrops of rock on surrounding islands. Some glittered alluringly in the sunlight but held nothing of value. The sailors explored onshore and found a narwhal preserved in ice. They decided it must be a legendary sea unicorn and harvested its spiral horn as a gift for Queen Elizabeth. Toward the end of July, the assayers found a band of black rock on the Countess of Warwick's Island (now Kodlunarn Island) where the ore was of high enough quality to turn a profit. The miners were put to work.

In the meantime, Frobisher questioned his captured Inuk about the five sailors who had disappeared the previous year. The man seemed to deny the accusations that the missing sailors had been killed, and Frobisher regained hope that they were still alive. A few days later, however, a group of sailors came across an empty Inuit summer camp where they found items of European clothing including a shirt, a doublet full of arrow holes and three odd shoes. Wondering if they belonged to the missing sailors, they reported back to their officers on board the ship.

The next day, the officers took a group of soldiers ashore in a different bay so they could approach from the hills and take the Inuit by surprise. Instead, they were surprised to find the Inuit camp had been packed up and moved. They marched on and caught sight of tents, but as they approached, the Inuit ran to their boats to escape. The soldiers fired after them and, with the help of more fire from an English boat on the water, forced them back to shore where a fight broke out. The Inuit's arrows and darts were no match for guns, but the Inuit did not want to be taken alive or dead. One injured Inuk flung himself from the rocks into the sea. Another followed him. The Englishmen supposed that the Inuit were cannibals who were afraid of being eaten by their captors and saw suicide as a more acceptable option. By the time half a dozen Inuit were dead, the others had escaped among the rocks, leaving only two women. The men were afraid that the older one might be a witch, so they let her go. The younger woman, who had her infant son strapped to her back, was taken aboard the *Ayde* to join the first captive. Frobisher was now worried that the Inuit left on the mainland would attempt a counterattack. He moved his soldiers from their ships to the camp onshore to protect the miners.

When several Inuit approached a few days later, Frobisher displayed the captives. He offered to exchange the woman and her baby for his missing sailors, and the Inuit seemed to agree. He sent the Inuit off with a letter for his men and also pen, ink and paper in case they could not appear in person. When the Inuit returned a few days later, they brought neither the English sailors nor a letter from them. They tried to trade goods, but the English were suspicious of their motives and refused. Over the next two weeks, the Inuït made several ambush attempts, perhaps to obtain hostages to trade for their young woman and infant. The English stayed in large groups and kept their mining camp well guarded.

By mid-August, the miners had gouged and pounded almost 200 tons of ore using sledgehammers, picks and crowbars. The ore was carried to the tenders, ferried out to the ships, lifted aboard and emptied into the holds. Some of the men had hernias (a common complaint of sailors), and others had gone lame. Their tools were broken and their clothes and shoes worn. Now ice was beginning to form around the ships each night. It was time to leave. The men packed up their tents, tidied the campsite and ferried their gear to the ships. They sailed out of the bay on August 24.

The October arrival of the *Ayde* and the *Gabriel* in Bristol caused great excitement, and the ore was moved to Bristol Castle for safekeeping. The *Michael*, separated from the others by a storm, returned to the Thames, and her cargo was moved to the Tower of London. Queen Elizabeth again appointed commissioners to oversee the treatment of the ore. When initial tests showed that worthwhile quantities of gold could be produced from it, Her Majesty was well pleased. With his dislike of books and figures, Frobisher left Lok to struggle with the accounts and find the money to pay the men's wages.

Over the following months, different assayers tested the ore and came up with alarmingly varied results, ranging from 13 ounces of gold per ton to none at all. The smelting process was producing a surprisingly high amount of slag. The head assayer, likely being pressured to produce more favourable results, complained that the smelting furnaces were too small and not hot enough.

The investors had already been asked to cover the shortfall in the salaries of the crew. As 1578 arrived, they were asked to pay for new furnaces. When the queen's commissioners decided that the assay results warranted an even larger expedition, the investors were expected to pay yet again. If they didn't come up with the money, their shares would be cancelled. The investors would not only lose any money they had already paid into the venture, but also their reputations as trustworthy businessmen and merchants. So, despite the assayers, who sneered at each other's techniques, and the highly controversial results, a larger expedition of 15 ships and 400 men was assembled to return to the mines.

Spies and Other Problems

The fleet sailed on May 31, 1578, with Captain Frobisher again on Her Majesty's ship the *Ayde*. The political implications of Frobisher's finds were percolating through Europe and Russia, and Queen Elizabeth knew she needed to strengthen her claim on the northern lands by populating them. The ships were carrying a prefabricated building because Elizabeth wanted three of the vessels to stay behind over the winter with 100 men. Only when they were settled, the mining operation underway, was Frobisher to continue his search for the Northwest Passage, and only then if he also watched for further outcrops of ore.

The Spanish, in particular, were very interested in Frobisher's activities, wanting to make sure that his expeditions did not infringe on Spanish territory. In addition, Spain controlled much of the world's supply of precious metals, which were being mined in Peru and Mexico. Gold was in great demand, both for currency and for investment purposes, and a large discovery of gold by the English would affect Spain's dominant position. To make sure they knew exactly what Frobisher found and where he found it, the Spanish planted a spy on one of his ships.

On this voyage, Frobisher sailed around the southern coasts of England and Ireland, making good time. However, with the vagaries of nature that make Arctic waterways navigable one year and impassable the next, the fleet found the route to Frobishers Streytes choked with ice. The sailors grabbed whatever they could to hang over their ships' hulls for extra protection and then lined up along the decks armed with oars and planks to fend off the ice floes. Ice ripped a hole in the *Dennys*, a 100-ton barque, and she sank with her cargo, although nearby ships were able to rescue all of her men. The *Judith* and the *Michael* disappeared and the sailors lost track of their position in thick fog. Frobisher, on the *Ayde*, sighted a headland and thought it was the entrance to Frobishers Streytes.

Christopher Hall and some other men disagreed and started an argument. Under cover of more fog, four ships turned back to what they thought were Frobishers Streytes. Determined that he was right, Frobisher sailed on for more than 160 nautical miles before he could bring himself to admit that he had made a mistake. He named the passage the Mistaken Straits (now Hudson Strait). Had Frobisher continued on along Mistaken Straits, he would have discovered Hudson Bay. As it was, he was a poor navigator, and his failure to fix his courses created confusion among mapmakers that ultimately resulted in errors on their charts.

Frobisher must have been sorely tempted to continue west through the wide-open waterway in hopes that he would reach the Pacific, but mindful of his instructions, he reluctantly turned around. The men were tired of pumping bilge water from their battered ships. Wondering how many times they could flirt with disaster before ending up at the bottom of the ocean, they began to question their leader's navigational skills. They wanted to go home. Defeat was not in Frobisher's vocabulary. He cajoled, threatened and made full use of his commanding presence, with the result that the captains sailed on to the Countess of Warwick Sound where most of the ships met up again.

They were considerably behind schedule when the men erected a mining camp on the Countess of Warwick's Island on August 1. Here, Frobisher used hard work and strict discipline to restore law and order among his men.

The discipline was necessary to keep track of all the ore and assays, keep them safe from a possible Inuit attack and to keep them healthy. They were not allowed to wash anything in the island spring that they used for drinking water and were only allowed to relieve themselves on the beach below the high-tide line where the tide would take care of the clean-up. The miners began to collect ore, the sailors emptied ballast from their ships and the first assays were made. The work was hard, the wind cold and the rain more often sleet or snow with temperatures only a few degrees above freezing.

Housing the colonists also posed a problem. Some sections of the prefabricated building had sunk with the *Dennys*, while others had been used as fenders against the ice. The carpenters claimed they didn't have enough time to build the missing parts, and the settlers' provisions were in the missing ships. When the captains learned that the colony's supply of beer had also gone astray, they decided that the settlers should return to England. However, they built a small stone house, leaving gifts inside for the Inuit, and planted grain, peas and corn outside. They wondered whether the house would still be standing when they returned the following year, or if the Inuit or the harsh weather would demolish it.

The men had only three weeks to complete the back-breaking job of mining and loading the ships with ore. Fuel for cooking was scarce and could not be spared for drying wet clothes or thawing frozen fingers. The arduous voyage, the inadequate nutrition and the daily fight against the cold began to take its toll. Some of the men collapsed from exhaustion and died. As provisions ran low and ice returned to the harbour, Frobisher debated whether to explore farther west along Frobishers Streytes. If he did so at this late date, the ships would have to wait out the winter frozen into the ice somewhere. Given the lack of provisions, the battered ships and the worn-out sailors, it seemed highly unlikely they would survive. Frobisher reluctantly reached the decision that, once again, Frobishers Streytes would have to wait.

On August 30, Frobisher briefed his captains for the return voyage. He ordered them to keep the ships together, to closely guard the ore and to unload the ore only at the new smelting furnaces at Dartford. If enemies took any of the ships, her officers were to throw all their charts and mining records into the sea before they were boarded. As each ship was ready to leave, she sailed out to Beare Sound, 16 nautical miles from the Countess of Warwick's Island, to wait for the others. Frobisher was still loading ore onto the *Gabriel* and the *Michael* when another storm began. The wind made it impossible for the men to return to their ships in their small boats, so they spent the night onshore. As the squalls grew more violent, the captains of the ships waiting in the sound worried that they would be blown onto the rocky lee shore. Some of them decided to leave and, unable to communicate through the storm, assumed that other ships closer to shore would pick up their share of the men. Others, like Hall in the *Ayde*, waited, but when the last ships failed to appear the following day, he decided that they must have passed unseen during the night. He set sail for England, too. In the meantime, Frobisher had squeezed the men left onshore aboard the overloaded *Gabriel*, as well as onto the *Michael* and a sailboat she was towing. Luckily, the last ships leaving the sound caught up to them and took the men from the small sailboat on board. Moments later, the sailboat sprang apart and sank, taking the men's belongings with her. The *Michael* and the *Gabriel* set sail for England.

With Frobisher's orders to keep close contact thwarted before the last ships had even left shore, they covered the lonely miles across the Atlantic where storms wreaked havoc with rotted rigging and weakened masts. Nevertheless, they all reached England except for the *Emmanuel*, which was trapped along the Irish coast by unfavourable winds, her masts broken and her sails torn. Her captain eventually beached her in a bay and stored her ore in some nearby buildings.

Through the first week of October 1578, one after another of Frobisher's ships limped into port, her men worn out and suffering from scurvy. Over 1,000 tons of closely guarded ore were pulled by horse and cart to Dartford for smelting. Frobisher would have been a hero but for the fact that no one could extract any gold from the ore. At first, people claimed that the metallurgist didn't know what he was doing or that the furnaces hadn't been designed properly. By the following February, however, excuses could no longer hide the fact that the ore was worthless. The assays performed under primitive conditions in the Arctic had been grossly inaccurate and the results lost in a mishap during the voyage back. By the time the investors received another hefty cash call to pay for the ships and the men's salaries, they knew the worst and didn't want to pay. Frobisher was unemployed and broke. His chance to find the Northwest Passage had passed.

Accusations of incompetence and fraud reverberated. The creditors wanted their money. Lok accused Frobisher of wasting money, misappropriating funds and not meeting the conditions of his contract. Frobisher demanded that Lok pay his and his men's wages for the last 17 months and claimed that Lok had been falsifying the financial records. This was later proven untrue, but as treasurer, Lok bore the brunt of the blame and was thrown into prison. He remained bitter for the rest of his life.

The question of whether the gold found in earlier ore samples was salted and the whole mining venture a hoax remains unanswered. Assaying methods were crude by today's standards, and fraud was common in Elizabethan England, but Lok would hardly have put himself in a position to lose his own money if he knew it was a scam. Frobisher, who hated financial wrangling and only appeared to find out that the ore was gold bearing when Elizabeth's secretary of state insisted he be told, also seems an unlikely candidate to think up such a scheme.

The Spanish spy remained undercover, and when King Philip heard that the ore was worthless, he lost interest in Frobisher's voyages. The next documented visitor to the Countess of Warwick's Island was an American, Charles Francis Hall, during his search for Sir John Franklin in 1861, almost 300 years later. An elderly Inuit woman recounted a story about five captured sailors who built a ship but sailed too early in the season. They returned with frozen hands, and the woman's ancestors helped look after them. When they recovered, they sailed away once more and were never heard from again. Charles Hall found the stone house perfectly preserved (thanks to the cold, dry climate and the lack of visitors to the island), right down to the dried peas, which now reside in the Canadian Museum of Civilization.

Frobisher's reputation and finances were in ruins. However, it's hard to keep a swashbuckling pirate down for long. His first wife conveniently died, leaving Frobisher free to marry another widow, Dorothy Wentworth. He provided for Dorothy in his will, so perhaps he was genuinely fond of her. It is likely that he returned to privateering for a time to recoup his losses.

Queen Elizabeth continued to challenge Spain's dominance, and in 1585 Frobisher helped Sir Francis Drake raid the Spanish colonies in the West Indies. When the Spanish eventually attacked England in 1588, Frobisher, who was in command of the *Triumph*, fought with his usual tenacity. The remnants of the defeated Spanish Armada fled, and the lord high admiral knighted Martin Frobisher on behalf of the queen.

In 1594, Frobisher led an attack on a newly built Spanish fortress in France and was shot in the thigh. By the time he arrived back in Plymouth, England, infection had set in. The wound was too high for the leg to be amputated, and without antibiotics to fight the infection, nothing could be done to save his life. He died on November 22, 1594.

2

Henry Hudson
(ca. 1570–1611)

BY THE TIME HENRY HUDSON, an expert navigator in his thirties, was ready to try his luck, others had already followed Frobisher to the Arctic. English navigator John Davis set off on his first voyage while Frobisher and Drake were raiding Spanish colonies in the West Indies. Davis didn't progress any farther than Frobisher, but his notes about the Arctic were so useful that the log of his third voyage was used as a model for a ship's log for the next three centuries. Seven years later, Dutch navigator Willem Barents sailed as far as Nova Zembla, an archipelago north of Russia. During his third voyage, in 1597, his ship became trapped in ice and Barents died trying to escape.

Hudson had a theory that the shortest route from

England to Cathay and the Indies was directly over the North Pole. He didn't know that the North Pole was covered with snow and ice. He assumed that Arctic summers would be much warmer than the winters because the summer sun didn't set. Davis' suggestion that ice could form only in fresh water or close to the mouths of rivers also supported the idea that the Arctic would be ice-free in summer. Hudson met with directors of the Muscovy Company and told them that he knew a secret route across the North Pole.

At the time, it took three years for one of the Muscovy Company's ships to sail to Cathay, load up with spices, silks, furs, incense and medicines and sail back to England. If they could reduce this time to one year by sailing a shorter route over the North Pole, then sailors' salaries and ship repairs would absorb less of their profit, and the men would have less time to grow mutinous or fall sick. There would be fewer opportunities for pirate attacks, and ships could avoid the violent storms around Cape Horn. The Muscovy Company directors decided to fund Hudson's expedition.

They supplied a small ship, the *Hopewell*, and Hudson hired a competent mate. It was hard to find a good crew willing to sail on a voyage of discovery. Sailors had to put up with inadequate food, crowded conditions, no washing facilities and a shortage of fresh water, as well as cold, wet watches with no warming fires. There were pirates to worry about, as well as storms, rats, lice, dysentery, typhus and, of course, scurvy. While the officers knew that scurvy was somehow related to diet, they didn't yet know how to prevent it, and many men died from scurvy on long voyages. Such hardships meant that men willing to sign on as crew were often criminals, drunks or unreliable characters who had trouble finding work elsewhere. Hudson hired nine other sailors, and his teenage son John joined the ship as cabin boy.

Walruses and Whales

On May 1, 1607, Hudson sailed down the Thames River from London. By June 13, he had passed the Faeroe Islands and Iceland and sighted the east coast of what he thought was Grønland (Greenland). Here, thick fog and winds out of the south forced him to change direction and steer northeast. The sailors tried to convince themselves that it was growing warmer, as popular theory predicted.

Beginning on June 27, they spent three weeks exploring the Spitsbergen archipelago where they saw large numbers of birds and seals, as well as an unusually large number of whales. In a sheltered bay at Collins Cape (named after Hudson's mate), there were whales everywhere. One swam under the *Hopewell* and hooked a fishing line that one of the crew had cast over the side. The whale took the hook and most of the line with him, but to everyone's great relief it did not damage the ship. They named the place Whales Bay.

They continued to sail northeast in a spell of warm, sunny weather that would have been reassuring but for the ominous increase in drifting ice. Just two days after leaving Whales Bay, they found the sea ahead blocked. Hudson could see no way through the mass of groaning, grinding ice. He had to swallow his disappointment and turn around.

As the sailors passed Collins Cape again, they assumed they were leaving the ice behind. But 11 days later they heard the roar of waves breaking on ice. Trying to peer through fog and rain, they were alarmed to see that the wind was pushing them westward toward an ice pack. Hudson ordered his men to lower the ship's tender, and tying it to the bow of the *Hopewell*, they tried to row her away from the ice. They bent their backs into it and heaved as hard as they could on the oars, but they continued to drift closer to the ice pack. Just when it seemed that the waves would batter them against the ice, the wind changed and a rare breeze out of the northwest blew up. The thankful men clambered back aboard the *Hopewell* and steered away from the icy trap.

On the way back to the Faeroe Islands, where Hudson stopped briefly to take on fresh water, he discovered an island inhabited by walruses and named it Hudson's Tutches. The *Hopewell* was now considerably farther west than she should have been. It's possible that Hudson was ignoring his orders by looking for signs of a passage to the west. If so, it was only a brief search because he sailed the *Hopewell* back up the Thames on September 15. After almost 20 weeks at sea, Hudson had failed to find a passage, but he had proved that there was no ice-free route over the

North Pole. He had also sailed farther north than any other documented explorer.

Like Frobisher, Hudson returned with unexpected treasure. He brought news of the large numbers of whales to be found around the Spitsbergen Islands, as well as the bounty of walruses at Hudson's Tutches. However, while Frobisher's treasure had ended up being dumped into the harbour or used to build stone walls, Hudson's treasure—whales—proved to be highly profitable. The blubber could be processed into lamp oil, and whalebone was needed to make stays for women's corsets. The Muscovy Company moved quickly to organize a whaling business based in the Spitsbergens. They asked Hudson to take charge, but he wasn't interested. He was determined to find a new passage to the East.

A Change of Plans
Anticipating a healthy income from whaling and walrus tusks, the Muscovy Company directors funded a second voyage; on April 22, 1608, Hudson set out again in the *Hopewell*. This time he intended to sail up and around the northern tip of Scandinavia, eastward across the Barents Sea, around Nova Zembla and along the northern coast of Siberia to the Pacific Ocean. The fact that this was the route Sir Hugh Willoughby had been searching for 55 years earlier didn't dampen Hudson's enthusiasm.

Willoughby and his entire crew had died aboard ship

in a sudden and strange manner that left everyone puzzled. Over 400 years passed before a medical historian figured out that, having stuffed portholes and chimneys closed, they probably had been poisoned by carbon monoxide from the sea coal they were burning to keep from freezing to death. In Hudson's time, however, the disturbing death ships were still a macabre mystery.

Hudson hired 11 men to join two returning sailors from his first voyage and his son John as crew. A tough, experienced but bad-tempered sailor named Robert Juet was Hudson's new mate, and the two men began to argue before the *Hopewell* even left the dock. Hudson was annoyed that Juet missed the blessing of the voyage on deck because he was too busy entertaining friends below. Juet grew upset when Hudson threw his friends off the ship so they could get underway.

The weather was bitterly cold. During the voyage, several of the crew had bouts of sickness made worse by their difficulty keeping warm. On June 15, two of the sailors saw a mermaid, something that was unusual but not unheard of. They described her back and breasts as having very white skin. Long black hair hung down her back, and her speckled tail was shaped like that of a porpoise. Hudson recorded the details in his ship's log.

The sailors spent several days dodging ice in the Barents Sea, once narrowly avoiding being trapped, and reached Nova Zembla on June 27. As Hudson began to search for a way around the northern tip of this land, he also sent groups of men ashore to fill water casks and find what they could to supplement their diet. They gathered birds' eggs and shot fowl. The sailors were not good hunters, and the deer and walruses they stalked usually got away. On the last night of June, their anchor failed and the ship ran aground. Luckily, they were able to pull her back into the water without damage, but that was as far as Hudson's luck went. He could not find a way through the ice, so on July 1 they began to look farther south.

Early one morning, the lookout shouted an urgent warning. A great ice pack was bearing down on the anchored *Hopewell*. The ship had one anchor set off her port bow and one off her starboard bow. Thinking quickly, Hudson stationed a man on each anchor cable. With one man hauling his anchor cable in, and the other letting his out, they were able to swing the ship from side to side to avoid large ice floes. The other men lined the decks and fended off ice chunks with poles and planks of wood. The men battled the ice for 12 hours until, suddenly, the ice pack passed. They went below to eat and then fell exhausted into their bunks.

Hudson couldn't find a way around the southern end of Nova Zembla either, but a wide river flowing through the middle offered one last chance. He turned the *Hopewell* northeast into the river. It was free of ice, but progress was slow because these were uncharted waters and he didn't want to run aground. To prevent this, Hudson sent Juet and half a dozen men to row the tender upriver and measure its depth. They used a lead line consisting of a lead weight attached to a line marked off in fathoms with knots (or pieces of cloth or leather) that could be felt in the dark. One man lowered the lead weight until it rested on the sea floor and then read the depth of the water by how much line he had let out. He could also pack a piece of tallow (fat) into a depression in the bottom of the lead to pull up a sample of the seabed and find out if it would be a good anchorage. Juet and his men returned the next day and reported that the river was too shallow for the *Hopewell* to proceed. Once again, Hudson's hopes were crushed. There was no way around Nova Zembla.

Realizing that the Muscovy Company might not fund a third voyage if he returned to England empty-handed, Hudson made a decision. If a northeast route to the Indies didn't exist, then he would search for a northwest route. John Davis had described a section of rough water with strong currents and high tides that Hudson thought might be an entrance to a northwest passage. It's not clear whether Hudson kept this new destination from his men because he knew they wouldn't want to go, or because he didn't think it was their business to know. He was a reticent man, ill at ease with these rough sailors, and his lack of leadership skills led to difficulties with his men on all of his voyages. This one was no exception; when the *Hopewell* turned west again, the sailors assumed they were going home.

On their return route, Hudson stopped to explore an island Sir Hugh Willoughby had charted. However, Willoughby's island had been recorded at the wrong latitude, and Hudson explored the wrong one. He claimed that Willoughby's island was shown too far north on his charts and this created further confusion (a common occurrence back then). The charts used by Frobisher had also placed land masses too far north, so when Frobisher reached Greenland he mistakenly thought it was a non-existent island shown as Frisland. Such mistakes were easily made in a land of frequent sea fogs with mirages that made land and mountains appear where there were none. With each explorer in turn renaming places, and islands being charted several times under different names and incorrect latitudes, the nautical charts were sometimes more hindrance than help. In addition, charts were occasionally doctored if an explorer wanted to disguise where he'd been or a merchant wanted to hide his secret source of valuable ivory tusks. Once they were made, mistakes could take centuries to correct.

Eventually, Hudson's crew realized that the *Hopewell* was not turning south toward England. Juet confronted Hudson, who admitted that he was taking them to North America. The sailors were tired of dodging deadly icebergs and eating biscuits full of weevils. They knew the weather would only get worse as the Arctic winter approached. The crew wanted to go home. They threatened mutiny and, knowing they could be hanged for their actions, coerced

Hudson into signing a letter stating that he was returning to England of his own free will. He had no choice but to do so.

They reached Gravesend on August 26 and said nothing about their disagreement. The directors of the Muscovy Company, disappointed with Hudson's failure to find anything profitable, refused to fund another voyage. Nevertheless, Hudson was determined to keep searching, and he approached the Dutch East India Company. As Spain and Portugal were losing their grip on their world trade monopoly, Holland was developing its sea power and was now England's main trading rival. The directors of the Dutch East India Company were also keen to shorten the long, expensive voyage around the Cape of Good Hope, but they weren't convinced that a northwest passage existed. While Hudson wrangled with the Dutch East India Company, the French began to show an interest. When the Dutch realized this, they relented and agreed to a fund a voyage. Perhaps they had heard about Hudson's single-mindedness and his habit of ignoring orders, because his contract was very specific. He was directed to look for a passage only to the north or northeast above Nova Zembla. If he could not find one, he was not to substitute another route.

Democracy Aboard the *Half Moon*

Hudson sailed from Amsterdam on March 25, 1609, aboard the *Half Moon*, a square-rigged ship of about 80 tons. She was 65 by 17 feet with an 8-foot-deep hold. The Dutch ships, built of pine, were narrower, lighter and faster than the stout oak English ships. The flat-bottomed ships also had room for more cargo, which gave them a definite advantage in the highly competitive business of trade.

Surprisingly, Hudson hired Robert Juet again as a member of the crew. His surly manner did nothing to help the English and Dutch sailors get along. Arguments and fights frequently broke out. Hudson was smaller and more complacent than Frobisher and did not have the latter's flair for discipline. To make matters worse, the Dutch sailors were used to sailing south to the Spice Islands. They found the bitter cold of the Arctic hard to endure. After battling unfavourable winds, strong currents and the inevitable ice during the first two weeks of May without making any progress toward Nova Zembla, the crew refused to battle their way north any longer. Once again, the peace-loving Hudson was forced to turn away from his goal. After his two previous voyages, however, he must have anticipated that his chance of success was slim. In a rare democratic moment, he put other proposals to his crew. They could look for Davis' Furious Overfall (now Hudson Strait) or they could explore a promising passage Hudson had heard about just north of the colony of Virginia. The crew voted for the milder climate of Virginia, and Hudson set sail for the New World, apparently unconcerned about the reaction of his Dutch employers when they found out.

The crew seemed happier as the *Half Moon* crossed

the Atlantic and sailed south along the east coast of North America. By mid-July, Hudson had reached Penobscot Bay, off the coast of Maine, and on September 2 they sailed into a magnificent harbour (now New York Harbour). From here they sailed upriver (now the Hudson River), hoping it would lead to the Pacific Ocean. Native Americans they met along the shores told Hudson that the river did not lead to an ocean, and when an advance party reported that the river ahead was only seven feet deep, Hudson realized it was not the passage he was looking for.

The journey back down the fertile river valley was eventful. The *Half Moon* ran aground twice, and the sailors continued to encounter groups of Native Americans. While some were friendly, others were not. As they set sail across the Atlantic, Hudson still wanted to explore Davis' Furious Overfall, but he realized that the Arctic was not a good place to pass the winter.

Hudson returned to Dartmouth on November 7, 1609, and sent a report to the Dutch East India Company asking permission to go on another voyage the following spring. Even though Hudson had disobeyed orders, he believed that the directors of the Dutch East India Company would likely be appeased by what he had found. However, when King James I, Queen Elizabeth's successor, heard that Hudson had made a major discovery for the Dutch, he was not amused. He placed Hudson under house arrest, and when Hudson was asked to sail to Amsterdam to meet with Dutch

East India Company representatives, he could not go. As the Dutch merchants planned the building of forts along the Hudson River to establish what they hoped would become a profitable fur trade, Hudson sat at home wondering if he would be thrown in jail or tried for treason. Fortunately, it was not against English law to explore under another country's flag. By spring, Hudson's friends had persuaded King James to allow the explorer to undertake another voyage, this one funded by a group of wealthy English merchants.

Mutiny on the *Discovery*

The *Discovery* sailed on April 17, 1610, with a crew of 22 men. Once again, the crew included Robert Juet as first mate and Hudson's son John. Also on board was Abacuck Prickett, one of the voyage's sponsors. Although Hudson could afford to hire good men for this voyage, he made some curious choices. At Gravesend he took on board Henry Greene, a sailor with a bad reputation. Only Hudson liked Greene, and rumours surfaced that the two men were lovers. Quarrels among the crew broke out almost immediately, and Juet spread the word that Greene was spying on the sailors so he could report any mutinous talk to Hudson. Given the dissent among Hudson's previous crews, Juet may have been right.

Hudson sailed for the Furious Overfall as directly as weather and sea conditions would allow. On June 25, they entered its surging tides and thick fogs. Impassable ice forced them south into a bay (Ungava Bay) where they sailed the *Discovery* back and forth for three weeks, like a big fish trying to stop the fisherman's net from closing around it. Frustrated by his inability to either advance or retreat, Hudson's usually calm temperament began to crack. His behaviour grew increasingly unpredictable and tempers flared. When the ship finally broke into clear water, Hudson offered to turn back. The men argued before agreeing to continue west.

At the beginning of August, they came to an island with an abundance of deer, cliffs full of birds and widespread sorrel (an edible green plant). The men wanted to stay a few days and stock up on fresh food, but Hudson refused. They had lost three weeks in the bay, and the short Arctic summer was almost over. His increasingly autocratic behaviour caused significant resentment among the sailors.

The coastline they were following took a sharp turn, and the *Discovery* followed it south for 300 nautical miles. When it finally began to curve west, Hudson thought he had found the much-sought-after passage. At last, he was sailing across the top of North America. But his excitement was short-lived. The coastline continued to curve until the *Discovery* was sailing north again. Instead of continuing to hug the coastline off his port side, as he had done since entering the Furious Overfall, he began to sail up and down James Bay. His indecisive wanderings alarmed his crew. Juet kept up a string of complaints and accusations that did little to help the situation. By the beginning of September, Hudson was tired of his first mate's disloyalty. He confronted Juet, who demanded a trial. This was a mistake on Juet's part; during the trial, the crew reported more than enough mutinous comments to hang him. Even so, Hudson added to the long list of mistakes he had made in dealing with his crew and merely demoted Juet, along with the boatswain who had encouraged him.

Hudson's wanderings continued, but as the temperature dropped, the ice began to build up. They would have to find a place to spend the winter. They chose a shallow, sheltered harbour (Rupert Bay) and set their anchor on November 1. Nine days later, they were frozen in. They had barely enough food to last until spring, so Hudson sent his men out to search or hunt for anything edible. With each day's meagre rations eaten and stomachs still rumbling, the men wished they were on the island full of deer, birds and fresh green sorrel where Hudson had refused to stop.

One of the men fell ill and died. His belongings were auctioned off among the crew, as was the custom, with the proceeds to be given to the dead man's next of kin. However, Hudson saved the man's warm coat for Henry Greene. Later, after Hudson argued with the ship's carpenter over the building of a house onshore—and then saw Greene go out hunting with the carpenter—Hudson grew angry. He took the coat back and gave it to Robert Bylot, his newly appointed first mate. The volatile arguments continued through the winter as the men began to suffer from scurvy.

By early spring, as the ice broke up, they were eating moss, frogs and anything else even slightly nutritious. In June, those who were well enough to work prepared the *Discovery* for departure. Amidst these preparations, Hudson demoted Bylot, whose navigational skills they had all come to rely on, and replaced him with a first mate who couldn't read or write. He also confiscated all the navigational instruments on board, as though he knew that trouble was on the horizon and wanted to make sure the men needed him to get home. They wondered if they were actually going home or if Hudson had other secret plans.

The *Discovery* weighed anchor on June 12, 1611, and in an effort to placate his unhappy and suspicious crew, Hudson shared what little food was left among the men. Some ate all their food at once; others tried to make their portions last. Over the following days, more arguments broke out. Hudson accused his sailors of hoarding food and searched their lockers. He confiscated the food that some of the crew had saved, which was rightfully theirs. The sailors claimed there were four cheeses missing and accused Hudson of hiding food for himself and his favourites. The men grew more desperate as they envisioned themselves starving in this desolate place.

On June 23, Greene and another man crept into Prickett's cabin and whispered their plan to take over the *Discovery*. Bylot was capable of navigating the ship back to England, but as most of the sailors were illiterate, they wanted Prickett to alter Hudson's log and to plead their case back in England. Prickett didn't like the plan, but he agreed to help, not wanting to be cast adrift with Hudson. At dawn, Hudson was tied up and hustled into the ship's tender with his son, three loyal sailors and four others who were too sick to help the mutineers. The tender was then cut loose.

Bylot sailed the *Discovery* home, reaching London on October 20, 1611. Five of the mutineers had died from injuries sustained during an Inuit attack that occurred when they were foraging for food. Juet, who was older than the others, was unable to keep himself alive by chewing on bird bones fried in candle grease. Although mutiny was a hanging offence, Bylot was pardoned due to his amazing feat of almost single-handedly sailing the *Discovery* home and for delivering Hudson's valuable chart marked with their route.

The following year, Bylot returned to what is now Hudson Bay with Thomas Button. Bylot and Button overwintered in the Arctic and spent two seasons searching for a passage leading west from the bay and for Henry Hudson and his men. They found neither, but Button was convinced that a northwest passage existed. In 1615, Bylot commanded his own ship with William Baffin as pilot. The two explorers decided that Davis Strait was a more likely waterway, and they discovered Jones and Lancaster sounds.

Despite these discoveries, investors shifted their interest from finding a new route to the East to exploring

Canada's resources. Later, in 1670, King Charles II issued a royal charter to the Hudson's Bay Company (HBC). This would lead to the establishment of England's lucrative fur-trading enterprise.

It was 1618 before the remaining mutineers were tried. The charge had not been clear and investors were placated by the hope that Hudson's great bay might turn out to be the Northwest Passage. After seven years, however, the authorities realized it was unlikely that Hudson and his loyal men were still alive, and they set a date to begin the trial. Prickett's report conveniently named the dead men as the major conspirators. There was ample evidence given of Hudson's erratic and inappropriate behaviour, and the accused men argued that they acted to avoid imminent starvation. After careful consideration, they were all released.

Later, explorers heard stories of a small boat found with dead Europeans inside and one survivor—a European boy. Explorers found a ruined house on Hudson Bay and the remains of a shelter on Danby Island. In the Ottawa Valley, the initials HH were found carved into rocks along the river. There were rumours of European men who married Native women, and a notebook was discovered that documented a grave marked "Henry Hudson" on one of the Spitsbergen Islands. However, no one actually saw him after he was cast adrift, and no one knows how Henry Hudson spent his final days.

CHAPTER

3

Samuel Hearne
(1745–1792)

SAMUEL HEARNE JOINED THE HBC in 1766 as first mate on the company ship *Churchill*, which was being used to develop a whaling base at Marble Island, north of Fort Prince of Wales. He had hoped to be promoted to captain when the position became vacant. Instead, he was asked to map the route to the Far-Off Metal River (said to flow through a copper mine), decide whether the river was navigable and determine whether the HBC would be able to build a fort there. He was also looking for a northwest passage.

The search for this elusive passage was now almost 300 years old. It had been sidelined during war and other momentous events. Spain and Portugal no longer monopolized the established routes to the riches of the Orient. Even so, the voyage was long and hazardous. Finding a northern passage had become something of a Holy Grail. Men were sure that it existed, and they wanted to find it. Samuel Hearne was particularly determined to do so and was well qualified to face the rigours of the North. At 24 years old, he was six feet tall, athletic and healthy. He loved snowshoeing, hiking and hunting, and during his six years in the British Navy, he had learned how to cope with deficient food and strict discipline. He was also adept at learning the languages of the local Inuit, Dene and Cree populations.

A False Start

Hearne set out from the fort on November 6, 1769, with Captain Chawchinahaw to guide him as far as Athapuscow Lake. Moses Norton, governor of Fort Prince of Wales, had told Hearne that another guide, Matonabbee, would meet up with them at this lake and take him on to the river through the copper mine. When several of Chawchinahaw's men disappeared one night with bags of Hearne's ammunition and other essentials, Hearne confronted the captain, who grew upset and said he could no longer guide the group. Chawchinahaw and his remaining men decamped, leaving Hearne and his four companions to pull heavily laden sleds 186 miles back to the fort. They arrived exactly five weeks after leaving, only to find another Native leader at the fort who also claimed to know the way to the river. Norton promptly hired this man as their guide.

Changing Fortunes

Hearne left for the second time on February 23, 1770. He mapped his route as the party tramped north, but disaster struck almost six months into their trip. Hearne was using a quadrant to calculate his position by measuring the height of the sun above the horizon. When Hearne stopped for lunch, he left the instrument in its stand so that he could take another reading after the break. While he was eating, a sudden gust of wind blew the stand over. The quadrant hit the stony ground and broke. Hearne stared at the shards of glass, unable to believe his bad luck. He did not have a replacement, and without this precious instrument he could not continue to map his route to the copper mine. Also, he would not be able to record the position of a northwest passage if he found one flowing out of Hudson Bay. There was little point in continuing on. The men turned around and began to retrace their steps to Fort Prince of Wales on the edge of Hudson Bay.

Now Hearne faced the humiliating task of telling Moses Norton that he had failed. Norton was like grit rubbing against Hearne's bare skin. The governor regularly told fort employees that they must practise virtue, but meanwhile he kept several local women for his own pleasure and pursued others who took his fancy, even married ones. Norton also drank and gambled, activities Hearne had no time for.

Hearne's bad luck continued the next day when a group of unscrupulous travellers visited his camp. When they learned that Hearne was returning to the fort, they declared that he wouldn't need his belongings and began to sort through them, taking items until there was nothing left. Vastly outnumbered and not wanting to antagonize the newcomers, Hearne pointed out that he would need such essential items as his knife, razor and a tool for mending his shoes. The newcomers gave these items back with the air of doing him a great favour before rifling through the belongings of his guides and companions. While this theft meant that Hearne and his men no longer had heavy packs to carry, the weather was harsh, and without even a tent for shelter, Hearne began to suffer from the cold. Each night he lay shivering before falling asleep exhausted.

Five weeks into the return journey, the thwarted explorers fell in with a group of Chipewyan travelling to the fort to trade furs. To Hearne's surprise he discovered that the leader of this group was Matonabbee, the man he had planned to meet up with on his first journey. When Matonabbee noticed Hearne shivering, he gave him a suit of skins to wear. He also said that he would be happy to guide Hearne to the copper mine if he still wanted to go there. By the time they reached Fort Prince of Wales on November 25, 1770, the two men had developed a mutual respect for each other.

Norton was not pleased when Hearne turned up 15 months early. In fact, Norton may not have expected to see Hearne ever again. He had sent him off twice with unreliable guides, and Hearne later found out that Matonabbee had never been asked to meet him and Captain Chawchinahaw at Athapuscow Lake. However, Hearne had given Norton his word that he would find the rumoured copper mine, and he was determined to keep it or die in the attempt. Besides, he wanted to find the Northwest Passage. He also had confidence in Matonabbee, and with an unusually trusting attitude, was willing to put his life in the chief's hands. To Norton's credit, he fitted Hearne out with everything Matonabbee suggested they would need. It is possible that Norton wanted Hearne to confirm his own suspicion that no western passage flowed from Hudson Bay, but he didn't like Hearne and didn't want to make it easy for him. Although he had two of the latest Hadley quadrants—one sitting unused—he gave Hearne an old, outdated quadrant to replace the broken one.

The Coppermine

Hearne left the fort on December 7, 1770, during a spell of fine winter weather. Matonabbee's party included his children and wives. The latter hauled the sleds, pitched the tents, made and mended clothing, cooked and kept him warm at night. Knowing that game would be hard to find in the area they were travelling through, Matonabbee and his men had cached some provisions along their route to the fort. Returning to the cache, nine days from the fort, they found that it had been looted. Every last scrap of meat and most of the tools had been taken. They had no choice but to trudge on with empty stomachs. Try as he might, Hearne could not banish thoughts of the excesses of past Christmases. When they finally had the opportunity to shoot some game eight days later, Matonabbee ate so much he made himself ill.

This was not the first time that Hearne had witnessed such behaviour among the Native peoples. They would endure days of hunger with no word of complaint, but when food was suddenly available they gorged themselves and then suffered for days afterwards. This swinging between feast and famine became a way of life for Hearne, too. Sometimes he existed for days on water, cranberries and a pipe of tobacco. When he did eat, it was often raw caribou brains, entrails and buffalo fetuses, or bites of caribou chewed by the women and then boiled into a kind of stew with stomach contents and water. The fresh meat and caribou stomach contents had enough vitamin C to prevent scurvy, and when these weren't available pine-needle tea did the job. Even Hearne had his limits though. He found the raw, malodorous meat of the muskox hard to eat and could not bring himself to swallow domestic lice or warbles (the fly larvae embedded in caribou skins). His companions ate these raw and said they were as fine as gooseberries.

The travellers endured an intensely cold February and tramped on. In April, they stopped briefly while one of the wives delivered a baby. As soon as the birth was over, the new mother strapped her baby onto her back and they continued on. The other women hauled the new mother's sled for the first day back on the trail, but on the second day she resumed this task. Hearne could see why Matonabbee chose his wives for their strength and size.

At Clowey Lake, they stopped to build canoes. There were no trees in the Barrens or in the tundra that lay ahead, and some of the rivers were too deep to ford. Over the following days, several groups arrived and insisted on accompanying the explorers. Among these was a man from whom Matonabbee had bought one of his seven wives a few weeks earlier. Now the man threatened to take her back unless Matonabbee gave him some tools, ammunition and other items he wanted. Matonabbee was outraged by the man's double-dealing and by his own loss of face. He told Hearne that his own people did not deserve to have him as their leader and would have to fend for themselves because he was leaving. He offered only to help Hearne find his way back to the fort. Hearne was dismayed. He had experienced bullying when he joined the navy at the tender age of 12 and had learned to deal with it using mediation skills over muscle power. Hearne now put these peacekeeping skills to good use. It took all of his well-honed powers of persuasion to talk his guide into continuing, but eventually he succeeded. They set off again on the last day of May. Hearne was unaware that more trouble lay ahead.

While canoes were being built, some of the newcomers were making what Hearne guessed to be shields. Wondering what was brewing, he asked his guide what they were for.

When Matonabbee told him that they would be used to deflect Inuit arrows, Hearne gradually deduced that his fellow travellers intended to massacre the Inuit who lived along the river near the mine, against whom they had a permanent grudge. He didn't know what to do about this. He tried to persuade the men to make peace with the Inuit, but they grew angry and accused him of cowardice. Concerned for his own safety, he rationalized that one man would be hard pressed to prevent a confrontation between mutual enemies. He would be powerless to do anything more than observe.

As they approached their destination, Matonabbee sent the wives and children off to a rendezvous point, accompanied by a few of the men. A group of about 60 men continued on with Hearne. Daylight hours were long, and there was plenty of game for food, but progress was slow, especially on days when the wind drove snow or sleet into their faces. Toward the end of June, Hearne met his first group of Yellowknife. They examined his fair skin and light eyes with great interest and told him that his long, blond hair was the colour of a urine-stained buffalo tail.

To Hearne's embarrassment, members of his group stole items belonging to the Yellowknife, as well as some of their women. Despite this, the Yellowknife guided them across the Stony Mountains, where they sometimes had to crawl on their hands and knees. It was impossible to start a fire in the continually wet weather, and they had no way to dry clothes or warm icy hands and feet. Discouraged, some of the newcomers turned back.

On July 14, 1771, Hearne finally stood on the bank of the river that, at his suggestion, became known as the Coppermine River. Despite reports that it was wide and navigable, it was full of shoals, rocks and rapids that HBC ships would be unable to navigate. Furthermore, the sparse, stunted trees would never provide enough wood for a fort.

Hearne's party moved on. They spoke quietly now and kept to low ground to avoid being detected as they closed in on the Inuit. Matonabbee wanted Hearne to wait out of harm's way, but Hearne was concerned about being killed by a fleeing Inuk and insisted on staying with his guide. They attacked at 1 a.m. The Inuit were asleep and were greatly outnumbered. They were butchered slowly with the obvious intent of inflicting as much pain as possible, including an old lady, fishing at some nearby falls, who didn't know what was happening until the men set upon her. It was far worse than any naval battle Hearne had fought, and he was appalled as he watched. When there were no Inuit left alive, the men plundered belongings, threw tents into the river and destroyed food supplies and anything else that might be of use to anyone who had escaped.

Hearne didn't have much appetite for his early breakfast of freshly caught salmon. Afterwards, the men walked the few remaining miles to the sea, where Hearne stood looking out over the islands and shoals of the Arctic Ocean—he was the first European to do so. He had walked for seven months through an Arctic winter, across spongy peat moss with sharp gravel that ripped his feet to shreds. He had waded through numbingly icy streams, been chased by screeching owls and had to smear his face with goose grease to ward off swarms of blackflies and mosquitoes. Yet, he had found nothing. He had not crossed any waterway that might be a northwest passage, and the Coppermine River was not navigable. Little did Hearne know that he was now looking at a section of the long-sought Northwest Passage. That discovery eluded him and remained for someone else to make. Instead of the excited satisfaction he had anticipated, he felt that all he had done was to bring death to the Inuit at Bloody Falls. He wondered whether his findings would ever be of use to anyone. Nevertheless, he claimed the coast by carving his name, the date and the HBC name on one of the Native shields. Then he placed it on a cairn near the mouth of the river.

He faced even more disappointment at the copper mine the next day. The man who had carried copper nuggets to Fort Prince of Wales, setting Hearne's long journey in motion, had claimed that the hills of the mine were made of lumps of copper, lying like pebbles for the picking. After searching for almost four hours, the group had found only one good-sized lump between them. It was time to go home.

The men were eager to meet up with their families and travelled hard, taking minimal rest. Hearne's legs and feet began to swell, and he frequently banged them against rocks. His toenails began to fester and drop off, and the skin on his feet was so badly chafed that his feet oozed with every step, leaving bloody footprints. He was in excruciating pain, but he knew that the Chipewyan wouldn't wait for him if he couldn't keep up. He had seen first-hand how they left their infirm behind with enough food and water to last only a few days. When he reached the women's tents on the last day of July, he bathed and dressed his feet. To his great relief, his feet healed somewhat while the group waited for everyone to meet up, although they remained tender for some time. It was another 11 months before Hearne arrived back at Fort Prince of Wales on June 29, 1772. He had crossed the frozen Great Slave Lake and part of the Mackenzie River system and had been absent for 18 months and 22 days.

At the fort, Hearne found that the nature of the fur trade was changing. The HBC's profits were falling, and competing traders had begun to intercept groups of hunters delivering furs to the forts. Now that Hearne had first-hand knowledge of the hardships of the journey faced by these hunters, he began to petition the HBC to build inland posts. He built the first of these, Cumberland House, and then in 1775, he replaced the deceased Moses Norton as governor of Fort Prince of Wales. He married Norton's mixed-blood daughter, Mary, and was happy until the French joined the United States in the American Revolution. On August 8, 1782, three French warships appeared in Hudson Bay with their guns trained on the fort.

Back when Hearne had joined the navy in 1757, England was one year into the Seven Years' War with France. His captain, eager for promotion, had taken every opportunity to engage French ships in what were often long and brutal battles. Hearne had been placed in command of the ship's guns and had seen, too many times, how cannonballs could mutilate a man's body. Familiar with the tactics of war, he also realized that the fort had no internal freshwater supply, and he knew that they could not survive a siege. He surrendered. Along with the other employees, he was taken prisoner, and the fort was blown up. His wife fled into the interior with the Chipewyan. It was a terrible winter, and the Native peoples had relied on the fort for food. Matonabbee eventually hung himself, and his family starved to death.

Hearne and his employees were herded aboard a ship captained by a French nobleman who had much in common with Hearne. The two young men liked and respected each other. As a result, Hearne was able to negotiate the release of his men along with a small HBC ship that they sailed back to Portsmouth, England. When the hostilities were over, Hearne was reappointed governor of the restored fort. He returned to Hudson Bay to find that Mary had died from starvation. He was devastated by the thought of her slow and horrible death. He ran the fort for another four years, but Mary lingered in his conscience.

After feeling ill for some time, he returned to England in 1787 and spent his last years rewriting his journal for publication. He suffered from dropsy (an accumulation of fluids in the body) likely caused by heart or kidney disease and died at the age of 47. His journal was published in 1795. While it was the source of great debate and criticism, his sketches, maps and descriptions contained a wealth of new information. Much of it was about animals, plants and the lives of the Chipewyan people. His geographical details, observations and maps helped to fill the empty spaces on the maps of the North.

4

John Franklin
(1786–1847)

JOHN FRANKLIN WAS SIX YEARS OLD when Samuel Hearne died. His first glimpse of the sea, at the age of 11, enthralled him and determined his direction in life. John was already developing into a serious young man with strong religious beliefs. His father, a grocer, wanted him to join the clergy. Nevertheless, when John turned 13, his father arranged for him to take a trial voyage on a merchant ship from the east coast of England to Lisbon, Portugal. He hoped John would find that life at sea was not nearly as glamorous as he imagined. It is possible that John's father also hoped the boy would be miserably seasick. Instead, John loved every minute aboard ship. As he enthused about his short voyage, gesturing wildly and grinning, his father realized that the youngest of his five sons was a born sailor. He began to enquire about possible positions, and in March of 1800, John signed up on HMS *Polyphemus*, just before his 14th birthday.

Switching between naval and merchant ships as opportunities arose, young John Franklin soon knew that life at sea would provide all the travel and excitement he could possibly hope for. He was marooned on a small and uncharted sandbar in the Torres Strait (between Papua New Guinea and the northern tip of Queensland), and he escaped French warships while returning from China. He fought in the Battle of Trafalgar in 1805, where he sustained a partial loss of hearing from the blast of firing guns.

As the Napoleonic Wars drew to an end, the British reduced their naval fleet of over 700 ships to 130. The seamen were paid off, and approximately 4,500 commissioned officers, including Franklin, were left ashore on half pay while their admirals considered various ways to employ their idle ships and sailors. Although Britain no longer needed a northwest passage, finding it had become a matter of national pride. Her people would never be able to sing "Rule Britannia! Britannia Rule the Waves!" again if the Russians were the first to sail the Northwest Passage. Sailors and scientists also wanted to understand terrestrial magnetism, which was essential to navigation, and to study electrical phenomena such as the aurora borealis (northern lights), which they thought must be related to this magnetism.

A Taste of the Arctic

Franklin made his first foray into Arctic waters in charge of a small whaling ship. David Buchan, sailing a second whaler, was in charge of the expedition. They had been commissioned to sail around the North Pole, through the Bering Strait and into the Pacific Ocean. Some of the sailors survived an attack on their longboat by a group of extremely aggressive walruses, and one of the ships narrowly missed being swamped by a calving iceberg. Finally, storms and ice damaged Buchan's ship so badly that he had to turn back. Franklin was forced to follow in case Buchan's ship broke up while he was still at sea. They arrived back in England in October 1818, barely six months after they had left.

A Second Chance

The following year, Franklin was placed in charge of his own expedition to map the Arctic coast east from the Coppermine River. Accompanying him were Dr. John Richardson and midshipmen George Back and Robert Hood, who were to note scientific data and make a visual record of the voyage using their artistic talents as modern explorers would use a camera.

Much of this naval expedition was overland, and while Samuel Hearne had completed a similar journey almost 50 years earlier, Franklin did not compare favourably with his predecessor. Hearne was used to the Arctic climate, physically fit, capable of shooting his own dinner and could communicate with at least some of the Native peoples. Although Franklin was only 33, he was unfit, overweight and had no idea what Arctic travel would be like. Some people claimed he would fail before the expedition began, and with only one month to plan and prepare, he certainly did make mistakes. Yet he was charming and enthusiastic, always kind to his subordinates, and he inspired loyalty.

He was assigned 19 men, and his flotilla of three ships sailed at the end of May 1819. He reached York Factory on Hudson Bay on August 30 and was fitted out with the largest of the HBC boats. Even so, his provisions were too bulky, and some, like the sides of bacon, had to be left behind. On September 9, his men began to sail, row, line and portage up the Hayes River. They reached Cumberland House in time to join in the customary Christmas dinner and dance. These celebrations were marred by devastating disease in the surrounding communities. Whooping cough and measles decimated the Native populations, and the survivors were often too weak to hunt or fish. A few were able to reach the fort where they were fed, but many starved to death.

At the beginning of the new year, Franklin travelled on to the North West Company (NWC) post at Fort Chipewyan on Lake Athabasca, where he had trouble finding voyageurs to accompany him north. Besides the terrible sickness that was spreading through the area, recent travellers had been attacked and murdered by hostile Inuit. Franklin also began to see signs of bitter rivalry between the men of the HBC and the NWC, on whom he was relying for supplies. By mid-June, the explorers were tormented by mosquitoes and could only escape them by filling their rooms with smoke.

By mid-July, Franklin had the manpower and supplies he needed and was able to press on to the NWC's Fort Providence, beside Great Slave Lake. Here, with the aid of interpreters, Franklin met with Chief Akaitcho of the Yellowknife, who agreed to provide guides and hunters for the expedition. They set off once more at the beginning of August in four canoes with supplies packed into 80-pound bales. They were now in Samuel Hearne's former territory. Anyone who travelled over this rough terrain burned a lot of calories, especially the voyageurs, who had to paddle the canoes and then carry them, along with the provisions, over the portages. They complained bitterly when the hunters could not supply enough food to satisfy their hunger.

At the end of August, the men built a winter camp with log houses and outbuildings that Franklin named Fort Enterprise. He sent men back to Fort Chipewyan and Fort Providence to see why their extra supplies had not been sent on to them. Franklin's men were told that the forts could not supply what they had promised. Although a few small shipments arrived, over the winter the explorers ate most of the dried moose meat and caribou tongues that were supposed to last through the next summer. There was also trouble with one of the interpreters. Franklin suspected that the man did not want to accompany him any farther and

John Franklin

Franklin's first Arctic expedition was sketched by Lieutenant Robert Hood as it crossed Lake Prosperous on May 30, 1820.
GLENBOW ARCHIVES NA-2821-8

that he was telling the Yellowknife and the voyageurs that the journey ahead was dangerous.

June brought warmer weather, and they continued on toward the Coppermine River, but the Yellowknife were nervous. When they encountered a group of Inuit near Bloody Falls, they decided to go home. Franklin could not change their minds, but he did extract promises that they would deposit provisions at Fort Enterprise and in a cache along the Coppermine River. Later that day, Franklin reached the shore of the Arctic Ocean and stood for a while thinking of his predecessor, Samuel Hearne. It was July 18, 1821.

Fed up with his interpreter's disloyalty and attempts to sabotage the expedition, Franklin sent him and four voyageurs back, instructing them to make sure the Yellowknife left the provisions as arranged. Then he led his remaining 19 men into the unknown.

The mapping took time, and the lack of provisions continued to plague the men. Franklin had hoped to bargain for food from groups of Inuit, but they hadn't seen any. When mid-August signalled that it was time to return to Fort Enterprise for the winter, Franklin considered his options. Retracing their route along the familiar coastline would be the easiest way, but they hadn't seen many animals or birds they could shoot. Concerned about feeding his men, he studied the map and decided to travel in a more-or-less straight line across the Barrens to Fort Enterprise.

The Yellowknife tried to avoid these lands that had no trees for fuel or protection, and with good reason. The journey from Point Turnagain (on the Kent Peninsula) soon deteriorated into a desperate struggle against starvation. Occasionally, one of the men would shoot a bear, a white fox or a muskox, but carrying heavy packs over frozen ground, with icy winds blowing through clothes stiff with frost, took a great deal of energy. The men picked lichen off rocks to try to assuage their gnawing hunger. One day they found a clump of Icelandic moss as they cleared snow to pitch their tents. They boiled the moss into soup, but it was so bitter that, starving as they were, they could only swallow a few spoonfuls. They found pieces of animal skin and bones left by wolves and boiled them up along with pieces of leather clothing and old shoes. As the men grew weaker, they abandoned items from their packs, leaving a trail of jettisoned books, magnets, compasses and other equipment they could no longer carry. They cut up the heavy tents. At night they lay on frozen blankets covered with pieces of tent canvas and slept in wet boots. They knew they'd never be able to force their swollen feet into boots frozen stiff by morning.

Franklin tried to keep his men together, but he knew that if they were going to survive the winter they had to get to food and shelter. Debilitated by scurvy, bowel complaints and starvation, the weaker members of the group had trouble keeping up. A few days into October, Franklin made the difficult decision to send four of the stronger men ahead, led by midshipman George Back. Franklin ordered them to kill or collect anything edible and to alert the Yellowknife to their desperate need for food. Two days later, two of Franklin's group went missing. Dr. Richardson retraced their tracks through deep snowdrifts and found one of the men lying unconscious. Behind his inert body, all footprints were blown over, and there was no sign of the second man. The doctor returned to the group to ask if anyone felt strong enough to go back for the unconscious man, but the others had reached their limits of endurance, and they struggled onward instead. When they came to a place with lichen to eat and willows for a fire, Dr. Richardson offered to stay with a couple of others and set up camp in the hope that the man left behind might regain consciousness, see their smoke and find them. The doctor urged Franklin's group to make haste to Fort Enterprise and send back help.

Franklin left a small barrel of ammunition with the doctor, hoping that mention of a gift might act as an incentive for the Yellowknife to help the struggling men. He also ordered those continuing on with him to empty their packs of non-essentials so they could travel as quickly as possible. Even so, the snow grew deeper than ever, and after only five miles they had to stop for the night. One man was having dizzy spells and another burst into tears. Three said they could not make it to the fort and asked if they could return to Dr. Richardson's camp in the morning to wait for help.

Franklin and his remaining companions struggled on, dragging one foot in front of the other. They tried to focus on the provisions that the Yellowknife and the voyageurs had promised to store at Fort Enterprise and on the blazing fire George Back and his men would have lit for them. But when they got there, there was no smoke rising from the chimney, no fresh tracks in the snow outside and no provisions. None of them could keep a stiff upper lip any longer. They sat in the icy fort and cried.

The only thing that was waiting for them was a note from Back, dated two days earlier, saying that he had gone in search of the Yellowknife. Taking some small comfort from this glimmer of hope, Franklin dredged up his composure. He announced that they would rest for a couple of days and then do likewise, but when he awoke the next morning he had to change his plans. The painful symptoms of scurvy included not only rotting gums and a body that slowly turned black from bleeding, but also swollen limbs. By now, Franklin's legs were so swollen that he could barely walk. Fortunately, some of the other men were more mobile, and they collected the lichen and old bones that kept all of them alive. With rest, the swelling in Franklin's legs began to go down, but he was still at the makeshift fort when one of Back's men arrived with a message. Back had written that he was unable to find anyone to help them, and he was wondering what to do next. Franklin surmised that Native families were likely making their way to Fort Providence and would be travelling slowly. If he set out for the fort, he might be able to catch up to some of them. He wrote a note for Dr. Richardson, and he instructed those too weak to accompany him to send food back to the doctor's group as soon as relief arrived.

Not far from the fort, Franklin fell and broke his snow-shoes. He was unable to make any kind of progress without them, so he told the others to continue on as planned while he returned to the fort. There he did his best to keep the men alive and their spirits up, but they gradually grew weaker. Desperately trying to keep warm, they began to demolish and burn the outbuildings. It was all they could do to carry the logs the 30 or 40 steps back to the main building. One day, they saw a herd of reindeer pass by, but no one had the energy to walk within shooting range. As they sat around the fire that evening they heard men in the outer room. For an instant, they imagined that it was the Yellowknife bringing food. Instead, it was Dr. Richardson and a companion bringing bad news. Of the eight men left behind, they were the only two still alive.

At Fort Enterprise, one man died and then another until it seemed unlikely that any of them would make it to Christmas. They didn't know that Back had found Akaitcho's camp until November 7, when a few Yellowknife arrived with some dried deer meat. Dr. Richardson warned the others to eat only a little at first because their stomachs were unaccustomed to digesting large quantities of food. However, their bodies desperately craved nourishment, and even the doctor was unable to stop himself from gorging. They all spent the night suffering terrible cramps. Two of the Yellowknife, familiar with the symptoms of starvation, stayed to care for the remaining men until they regained enough strength to begin their long journey home.

Only nine of the 20 men made it back to England alive the following year, but strangely, Franklin was greeted as a hero. The grim details of his Arctic journey captured the interest of the Victorian population, and Franklin began to appear in poems such as Samuel Taylor Coleridge's "The Rime of the Ancient Mariner" and in gothic novels such as *The Frozen Deep* by Wilkie Collins. In addition, Franklin wrote his own account of the voyage. The book sold well, and he became known as "the man who ate his boots."

Franklin recovered and began courting Eleanor Porden, a 25-year-old poet he had met before his first brief Arctic voyage. He married Eleanor on August 19, 1823, just a few months after his father's death. Although Eleanor had tuberculosis, the following June she gave birth to a daughter whom they named Eleanor.

The British were determined to resolve the question of whether or not the Northwest Passage existed, and the Admiralty planned a simultaneous assault from different directions using four veterans of Arctic exploration. Frederick William Beechey was to sail north through the Bering Strait between Russia and Alaska and then turn east to make his way along the Arctic coastline. George Francis Lyon would sail to Repulse Bay, off the northwest coast of Hudson Bay, and then travel west, overland, to Point Turnagain. William Edward Parry was to sail Lancaster Sound leading west out of Baffin Bay, continue on into Prince Regent Inlet and look for a route heading west. John Franklin and his men were to travel along the Mackenzie River to the Arctic Ocean and then split into two groups to explore the coastline both east and west of the river mouth.

Success at Last
Wanting to avoid the pitfalls of Franklin's previous expedition, the Admiralty spent a year planning both the route and the provisioning details. They allocated a larger contingent of men so that Franklin would not have to rely on

unwilling or unreliable local help. The Admiralty also had four boats built for Franklin's use. The fact that both Dr. John Richardson and George Back were willing to return to the Arctic with Franklin, after witnessing his questionable habit of blindly following orders and his dangerously limited understanding of Arctic survival tactics, reflects how they felt about the man.

While preparations were underway, Eleanor's health deteriorated. Giving birth had been hard on her weakened body, and doctors had not yet discovered antibiotics or any other cure for tuberculosis. With Eleanor now confined to bed, and the fact that Franklin had almost died on his previous trip, it's a wonder that he agreed to go at all. However, Eleanor insisted that their marriage should not interfere with his career. Franklin left England on February 16, 1825, and eagerly awaited a letter from his wife. Instead, he learned that she had died barely six days after his departure. Swallowing his sorrow, he continued to carry out his orders and left the care of his infant daughter to his sisters and family friends until his return—whenever that might be.

The planning paid off, and Franklin's men were able to map a long section of coastline. They returned to England in September 1827 in reasonable health after a two-and-a-half–year absence. While none of the Arctic veterans had joined up with each other as the Admiralty had hoped, and the existence of a passage was still in question, Franklin's expedition was considered a success.

On to Warmer Climes

Franklin again published his findings, and the following year he was knighted by King George IV for his service to king and country. He also married Jane Griffin, who had been a friend of his first wife. Jane was a dynamic and adventurous woman who would have approved of her new husband undertaking another Arctic expedition. However, the Duke of Clarence, soon to become King William IV, had recently been appointed lord high admiral. He often made decisions on a whim, and he would not recommend that Franklin return north. After two years of domesticity, Franklin was sent on a three-year tour of duty in the Mediterranean. When this ended in 1833, he was again placed on half pay and found himself at loose ends. He applied for a diplomatic post and in 1836 was appointed lieutenant governor of Van Diemen's Land (now Tasmania).

Britain had been sending convicts to Australia since 1787 and to Tasmania since 1803. The previous governor had taken a totalitarian approach, controlling the convicts (almost half of the colony's population) by treating them harshly. Franklin was more humane and loathed the severe punishment handed out—sometimes unjustly—in the name of discipline. He tried to curb corruption and worked toward a free and self-governing colony. This caused friction among the previous governor's associates, who were politically connected and helped to run the colony. Lady Jane Franklin tried to help her husband but was accused by others of interfering. The strain

between Franklin and the Colonial Office reached the breaking point seven years into his appointment, and he and Lady
Franklin were sent home in 1843.

Two years later, when Sir John Franklin turned 59, he
should have been thinking about retirement. He had out-
lived all of his brothers and was well past the average life
expectancy of the time (35 to 40 years). However, Franklin
was a restless man who had the recent blot of his dismissal
on an otherwise distinguished record. His memoirs were
already written, and the thought of spending his remaining
years playing bridge and drinking one too many brandies at
his club only added to his obsession with finding the elusive
Northwest Passage.

Return to the Arctic

Luckily for Franklin, or so it seemed at the time, King
William had died. Queen Victoria had begun her long
reign and, along with the first sea lord, was persuaded
against leaving the final section of the Northwest Passage
for some other nation to find. The British were proud of
their technological prowess and determined to dispatch the
best-equipped polar expedition ever. Two sailing ships, the
Erebus and the *Terror*, were fitted with the latest invention—
screw propellers driven by steam engines. Their bows were
reinforced with sheet metal to help them move through ice.
John Harrison, an Englishman, had designed a clock that
could keep time accurately at sea, and the navigators would

be able to use this to calculate their position of longitude. The provisions were cooked and canned to keep out mould and maggots. The expedition was even issued with leather goggles to prevent snow blindness. Recent expeditions had filled in many of the blank spaces on the maps and charts— only one section of uncertainty remained. With the right person in charge, the expedition would surely succeed.

The Admiralty's first choice of commander was Sir James Ross. However, Ross had recently promised his young wife that he would not sail on any more voyages of exploration. The ambitious Lady Franklin wanted no such promise from her husband; but with much of his hair gone, his waistline larger than ever and a shortness of breath that was obvious even when he was sitting down, his suitability was questioned. The lords of the Admiralty suggested that perhaps he was too old, but Franklin's friends and fellow explorers insisted that he would die of disappointment if he was not offered the job. The appointment was made, and Franklin sailed from the Thames on May 19, 1845. His ships held 132 sailors and officers and enough food to last three years. His instructions were to sail west through Lancaster Sound and Barrow Strait, then turn south and west at Cape Walker.

On July 26, 1845, whalers spotted the *Erebus* and the *Terror* tied to an iceberg in northern Baffin Bay—presumably waiting for the ice to clear from Lancaster Sound. Then, without a trace, the two ships disappeared.

5

John Rae
(1813–1893)

WHEN JANUARY 1847 ARRIVED WITHOUT any word of Franklin's two ships, his wife and friends began to worry. Now that there were whaling ships, voyageurs and HBC and NWC trading posts visited by fur traders and groups of Native peoples, news got around. It was odd that no reports of contact or sightings had filtered back to England.

In the meantime, following their original plan, the lords of the Admiralty were preparing to send a supply ship to meet the triumphant Franklin in the Beaufort Sea. In addition, they had a contingency plan for a rescue party, in case something went wrong. They were already assembling a search party at the HBC's York Factory. Franklin's long-time friend Dr. Richardson, now Sir John Richardson, was standing by to lead it. He would need a second-in-command and had no shortage of gentlemen eager to fill the position, but none of them were qualified. Then, Richardson read an article in the daily newspaper written by John Rae, a young man who had recently returned to Britain after surveying 600 miles of Arctic coastline. He was perfect for the job.

Rae had grown up in the Orkney Islands, off the northern coast of Scotland. By the age of 20, he was a qualified surgeon. He was also extremely fit, skilled at shooting game and experienced in handling the family's small sailboats in the storms that often blew up around the islands. The sight of HBC supply ships calling in at Stromness for fresh water and provisions was a familiar one, and his father and two of his older brothers were already working for the HBC. It seemed only natural that Rae should sign on, too. In June 1833, he sailed to Moose Factory in James Bay as surgeon on the HBC supply ship *Prince of Wales*, intending to work one round trip to see if the life suited him. Rae's visit should have been a short one. After 17 days onshore while provisions were unloaded and furs bound for Britain were loaded, the *Prince of Wales* left for the return journey to Scotland. However, the captain couldn't find his way through the mass of ice blocking Hudson Strait. He knew that resources at Moose Factory would be severely stretched if the post had to feed his crew and passengers all winter, so he sailed to an abandoned post on Charlton Island where they could hunt for themselves.

Rae remained in good health and took up snowshoeing to keep physically fit and because it was the only way he
could hunt in deep snow. What little game he found was a
welcome supplement to their diet of salt meat and biscuits,
but some of the men began to suffer from scurvy. Rae knew
there was something in fresh fruit and vegetables that would
prevent this horrible illness, but they didn't have access to
any fresh produce. Instead, he followed a Native remedy and
brewed spruce-needle tea for the men to drink. Even so, several of them grew seriously ill. The captain and his first mate
were the worst off. The captain's legs began to swell while the
first mate slowly turned black from internal hemorrhages.
As the collagen in their connective tissue, bone and dentin
broke down, their body cells literally became unglued. They
began to rot, giving off a revolting smell. Luckily, Dr. Rae
had a strong stomach. He stoically nursed the two men as
they died.

As spring arrived, Rae gathered wild pea shoots to feed
to his other patients. Then one day, beneath the thinning
snow, he found buried treasure—a patch of wild cranberry
bushes with last summer's berries still attached. It was too
late to save the captain and first mate, but the other men
began to recover as they ate the shrivelled berries, which
were rich in the vitamin C that their bodies craved.

When the ice cleared in July, the men hauled the *Prince
of Wales* back into the sea and sailed to Moose Factory. The
post's governor, impressed with this resourceful young

doctor, offered Rae a position as clerk and surgeon at the factory. Rae was beginning to like this wild new country, and the harsh living conditions didn't bother him at all. He had a remarkable tolerance for being wet and cold, and his fit, wiry body could keep functioning on minimal nourishment. He agreed to stay for two years. Ten years later he was still there.

By the spring of 1844, Rae knew a great deal about the fur trade. He had also learned a lot about travelling in the North. His patients included Native and Métis people, and Rae became renowned for the speed and distance he could travel on snowshoes. He also attracted the attention of HBC governor Sir George Simpson.

Governor Simpson and the other HBC directors wanted the glory of finding the Northwest Passage. Two surveyors had begun a survey of the northern coast of Rupert's Land in 1839 but were interrupted by bad weather and the subsequent death of one of the surveyors. With Rae's exceptional physical prowess and his ability to travel light and live off the land, he seemed the perfect candidate to complete the survey, except for one small problem: he didn't know anything about surveying. Simpson sent Rae to the magnetic observatory in Toronto. Here Rae learned how to use a sextant and accurately record his location. Then, in the summer of 1845, he retraced his way north. As with Franklin's first overland Arctic expedition, many men thought Rae would never return from his surveying trip, and they didn't want to accompany him. However, Rae insisted on taking only two small sailboats and 12 men. By the time he reached York Factory in the fall, he had all but two of the men he needed.

Rae's First Surveying Trip

On June 13, 1846, Rae and his men sailed from York Factory in two 22-foot York boats, the *Magnet* and the *North Pole*. At Fort Churchill, Rae hired two Inuit hunters and continued on. While the men might have been apprehensive at being the first Europeans to set off on a 15-month expedition with provisions to last only four months, Rae's expedition was not like those of other explorers. Because they intended to find their own food, they would not have to race to reach their goal and return home before food ran out. They would pull their tents on sleds instead of carrying heavy packs, and when spring arrived and they could no longer use the sleds, they would leave the tents behind and build shelters. Governor George Simpson and John Rae were both contemptuous of the navy's "gentleman" explorers, who burdened their parties with silverware for afternoon tea and could cover only a few miles a day. Rae believed that a true leader should be self-sufficient and able to outperform his followers.

Even with Rae's efficient and practical attitude, the surveying required a lot of stamina. The men had to cross a series of icy ridges, climbing up one side and sliding down the other while trying not to skid into large rocks. Sometimes they sank up to the waist in snow. The spring sun turned the snow wet and heavy, and it clung to snowshoes and sled runners, forcing the men to travel at night. Nevertheless, they returned to York Factory on September 6, 1847, a little thinner but in good health and spirits and with bags of spare pemmican (dried meat pounded into a paste with melted fat). Rae had surveyed 600 miles of coastline, proving that Boothia was a peninsula rather than an island and that no channel cut across this peninsula to form part of a northwest passage.

York Factory was bustling when Rae and his men returned. The HBC supply ship had arrived bringing 20 extra soldiers and sailors with four small boats to help search for the Franklin expedition. The ship also carried a letter for Rae from Governor Simpson. Rae read that he had been promoted and could take a leave of absence until the annual council meeting the following June. It had been 14 years since Rae had left Scotland for what he thought would be a few months. His father and one of his brothers had since died. Rae decided it was time to visit his mother and caught the supply ship home.

While Rae spent time with his mother and visited friends and relatives, Sir John Richardson asked if he would join the search for Franklin as his second-in-command. With the entire nation speculating over what had happened to the Franklin expedition, Rae could hardly refuse. He sent his apologies to Governor Simpson for changing plans so abruptly and turned his thoughts to the search ahead.

Searching for Franklin

Now that the lords of the Admiralty had finally agreed that Franklin and his men might be in trouble and need help, the big question was where to look for them. Even with modern satellite communication and global positioning systems, it's possible to lose a small airplane in the mountains or a sailboat in a round-the-world race when its position was known only a few hours earlier. Imagine, more than 150 years ago, trying to decide where to look for two 100-foot ships that were last seen three years earlier in Baffin Bay. Everyone had an opinion, and the possible search area was vast. The Admiralty decided that two ships led by James Clarke Ross would approach from the east and sail through Lancaster Sound. Another two ships would approach from the west, while Rae and Richardson were to travel overland to the Coppermine River and search along the coastline and Wollaston Peninsula.

The two men left Liverpool in the spring of 1848, travelling to New York and then Montreal by steamship. From there they paddled along the fur-trade route, each in a canoe with eight voyageurs, for 13 or more hours a day, interspersed with portages of varying difficulty. While this was easy for Rae, who had often travelled alone, it was harder on the 61-year-old Richardson, who had long since retired from such jaunts.

At Cumberland House on the Saskatchewan River, they met up with the 20 soldiers and sailors from York Factory who were to accompany them. Rae was dismayed by their reluctance to exert themselves and their lack of physical stamina. They began to journey north, but these men refused to carry anything but light loads over portages, and Rae found their progress painfully slow. He and Richardson had planned to cross Union Strait to Wollaston Peninsula before winter. Rae chivvied the men along as best he could and, when setting a good example did not have the desired effect, threatened to leave behind any who couldn't keep up. This was more effective. Even so, they ran out of time and had to spend the winter at Fort Confidence on the mainland, where Rae and Richardson occupied themselves by recording meteorological observations. In May 1849, the two men parted company. Richardson had experienced heart spasms during the march to the fort and was returning to England. He left two men to look after the fort and six to continue the search with Rae. They had until August 25 to find some sign of Franklin, and then Rae's orders were to travel to Fort Simpson and resume working for the HBC there.

Rae watched for an opportunity to sail across Union Strait, but was frustrated when spring breakup came late; by August 23, he had run out of time. He travelled to Fort Simpson where he took charge of the Mackenzie River district headquarters, but after three years of travelling, he couldn't settle down to the paperwork of the fur-trade business. His unsuccessful search rankled him, and the years were rolling by. Maybe it was time to find a wife—a British wife. Rae wrote to ask for leave the following summer. The busy winter trading season would be over, and he could try his luck courting.

The other searches for Franklin were dismal failures, too. Ross' ships were trapped twice. By the time he'd worked them out of the ice for the second time, he'd had enough and returned to England. The ships approaching from the west were still searching but had found nothing. Lady Franklin played on the sympathy of the British and American public, urging anyone with influence to keep searching. The Admiralty offered a reward to anyone assisting members of the lost expedition and was under increasing pressure to find the missing men. As a result, Rae did not receive permission to go home for the summer of 1850. Instead, he was told to resume his search. He spent the winter at Fort Confidence and during the spring and summer of 1851 covered a considerable area of coastline and Victoria Island, surveying and making notes as he went. Three times he attempted to sail across to King William Land. Had he been able to make the crossing, Franklin's story might have ended differently. As it was, Rae was stopped by ice and adverse winds. He did find two objects of interest, however—a man-made pole and another piece of oak. Both had obviously come from a British ship. Could they have come from one of Franklin's ships? When time ran out, Rae was determined to take his leave. He journeyed home, carefully packing these pieces of a ship to show the Admiralty.

While Rae was in Scotland, the Royal Geographical Society awarded him their Founder's Medal for his surveys of Boothia Peninsula and the coast of Victoria Island. Governor Simpson also asked him to plan another surveying expedition. The unmapped section of Arctic coastline was shrinking yearly. The last piece of the Northwest Passage, if there was one, was about to fall into place, and the directors of the HBC were determined to find it. Rae left for York Factory early the next year, still without a wife, but now with thoughts of retirement after this final surveying trip. He would turn 40 in September, and although he was still exceptionally fit and loved shooting and walking, he couldn't tolerate cold weather the way he used to.

An Unexpected Find

In the last week of June 1853, Rae left York Factory with a few men and sailed on to Fort Churchill to hire an Inuit interpreter. He had hoped to complete his survey before winter arrived, but delays due to bad weather made this impossible. Rae returned to Fort Hope in Repulse Bay, where he had built a stone house during his first Arctic expedition. He didn't intend to live in the house, as he had long since learned that the snow-block houses built by the Inuit were much cosier and could be put together in an hour. However, he was curious to see whether any groups of Inuit had made use of it. They were known to eat food that others had cached, take stored items that took their fancy, dismantle boats for useful pieces of metal and burn the wood if they wanted a fire. While there were signs that the Inuit had visited the stone house, Rae's party was unable to make contact with them. Rae had been hoping to buy dogs for their overland travel, but now it looked as though they would have to pull their own sleds. Rae had them rebuilt into a lighter and more practical design.

Four men left Fort Hope with Rae on the last day of March 1854. The other three stayed to guard their belongings, especially their boat. Rae's party struggled through snowstorms and bitterly cold temperatures, sometimes covering only a few miles a day. In mid-April, they met up with an Inuk who was driving a dog team. Rae hired the team's services for two days and was loading belongings onto the dogsled when a second man with more dogs offered to join them. The Inuk was wearing a gold cloth band that looked like it had come from a naval officer's cap. Through his interpreter, Rae asked about the gold band. Rae was told it had come from the place where a group of white men had starved, but that he hadn't been there, couldn't take them there and couldn't point out the place on a chart. Rae wondered if it had come from one of Franklin's officers' caps, so he bought the gold band from the Inuk. The thought of finding out what had happened to Franklin was tempting, but the information seemed too vague to act upon, and after nine years, it was unlikely that any of the men were still alive. Before Rae parted company with the two Inuit,

he asked if their people could bring any other relics they
possessed to his winter quarters in Repulse Bay.

Rae pressed on along the west coast of Boothia Peninsula,
where he noticed that the coastline did not agree with his
charts. He studied the landmarks and lined them up, check-
ing his position carefully. A flicker of a possibility began to
emerge. He was supposed to be looking out over land, but
this wasn't frozen land—it was ice. Rae had learned to rec-
ognize different kinds of ice, and this ice looked as though
it had formed over water and would melt when summer
arrived. This would open up a navigable passage between
King William Land and Boothia Peninsula. It would make
King William Land an island! He was sure he had discovered the middle section of the Northwest Passage. He made
careful notes and built a cairn to claim what he had found.

Rae returned to Fort Hope, where Inuit families were
arriving with relics to trade and news to tell. Items he
bought from them included an engraved gold watch, a
small silver plate engraved with Franklin's name and one of
Franklin's medals. Rae spent days questioning the visitors,
hoping their answers might explain what had happened to
the expedition. As he heard details of mutilated corpses
and human remains found in cooking pots, a horrible suspicion grew into certainty. In a drastic attempt to satisfy
their starving bodies' craving for food, some of the men
had resorted to cannibalism.

From the descriptions, Rae had a good idea of where

the remains were, but it was too late to travel overland on snowshoes because the ice was melting. He hadn't had much luck sailing a small boat across to King William Island, either. His only way to get there would be to wait until freeze-up again in the fall. In the meantime, other searches were setting off in the wrong direction and risking more lives. He decided to return to England as he had planned and report his discoveries in person.

The lords of the Admiralty received Rae as soon as he arrived in London in October of 1854. They had spent a great deal of money sending search-and-rescue ships, some of which had become trapped in ice. Now they were forced to send more ships to rescue some of the rescuers and were using resources needed for the Crimean War against Russia. With Rae's indisputable proof that Franklin and his men were dead, they were glad of the opportunity to bring closure to the whole sorry affair.

The following day, a letter Rae had written to the editor about his recent discoveries appeared in the daily newspaper. The editor also published a much more detailed report that Rae had considered unsuitable for the general public and had written for official eyes only. His conclusion that cannibalism had been committed brought outrage. The questions of who leaked this information and for what purpose remain unanswered. The public, and especially Lady Franklin, were incensed.

Ironically, this was not the first time cannibalism had

occurred in the course of one of Franklin's expeditions. During the first disastrous overland expedition of 1821, Dr. Richardson had shot a starving Iroquois whom he found cooking human body parts. The few men who knew the truth kept it quiet. This time the secret was out. The British were proud of their nautical prowess and their empire. They did not want to believe that this could happen among British officers in Queen Victoria's time.

Lady Franklin was determined not to allow such terrible accusations to besmirch her dead husband's honour. She began a long, vindictive campaign to discredit Rae. She also claimed that her husband had discovered the Northwest Passage. Arguments erupted everywhere. Ironically, Robert McClure had recently been knighted and awarded the £10,000 prize for discovering the Northwest Passage, although he hadn't actually sailed it because his ship was frozen into the ice. After being trapped for three years, McClure and other survivors, including one who had gone mad, were in bad shape when they were rescued. Even so, McClure refused to share his prize money with his rescuers, stating that he hadn't needed their help.

Unsolved Mysteries
Franklin's defenders accused the Inuit of being liars and insisted that Rae should have checked their story instead of rushing back to England to claim the reward offered for news of Franklin. Some argued that if the Inuit could

survive in the Arctic then so could Franklin, and his men wouldn't have needed to resort to such behaviour. Others claimed that the Inuit must have cannibalized the bodies because British sailors would never do such a thing. Rae's maps were copied and the work was attributed to explorers outside the HBC. Rae had to fight to obtain the prize money for establishing Franklin's fate. He was eventually paid but was never knighted as other explorers were who had contributed much less to their country.

Rae spent the rest of his life trying to re-establish his integrity. At the age of 46, he married 21-year-old Catherine Thompson. They travelled between Britain and Canada, and Rae practised medicine and delivered talks. In 1864, he led a survey for a telegraph line from Red River to the Pacific coast. He slowly regained some respectability, and he remained incredibly fit into his late 70s. He died in London on July 22, 1893, and was buried in the churchyard of St. Magnus Cathedral in Kirkwall.

Lady Franklin, still looking for answers, bought a boat for Francis McClintock, who sailed north in the spring of 1859. While he confirmed Rae's reports and agreed that Franklin had found the Northwest Passage, he raised more questions. He found a partially dismantled cairn at Cape John Herschel on King William Island and was convinced that Franklin's expedition records had been removed. But by whom? The Inuit would not have had any interest in written papers and would surely have demolished the rest of the cairn looking for objects of value. He wondered if one of Franklin's would-be rescuers, perhaps even Rae, had visited the cairn. If so, what secret were they keeping?

More than 150 years have passed since Rae heard the news of Franklin's dead men, and yet experts are still trying to piece together what happened. If Rae had made it across the strait to King William Island in 1851, he may well have discovered valuable records. As it was, the remains were looted and no official expedition records have ever been found. Notes left in cairns along the coast indicated that the expedition was still in good shape two years after it left England but that on June 11, 1847, Sir John Franklin died. Spring break-up never came, and instead of the *Erebus* and the *Terror* being released, they drifted south still trapped in the ice. The ships were undamaged, but the men began to fall ill and needed fresh food to fight scurvy. Franklin's successor took a group of men south on foot to find caribou and other game. As they dragged a small boat and other belongings loaded onto sleds, they died in ones and twos along the way.

In the 1860s, American Charles Francis Hall visited King William Island and collected convincing eyewitness accounts that agreed with Rae's reports. In August 1967, the Canadian Department of National Defence searched King William Island for Franklin's grave and records of his expedition, but was unable to find either. Divers searching for the *Erebus* and the *Terror* found only debris from an old wooden ship that may or may not have been one of Franklin's.

In 1984, a scientific team led by Dr. Owen Beattie, a forensic anthropologist at the University of Alberta, exhumed the bodies of three men who had died early in the expedition and been buried on Beechey Island. The bodies had been well preserved in the frozen ground, and strangely, an autopsy had been performed on one of them before burial. Beattie's analysis showed that the men had suffered from lead poisoning caused by improperly canned food. Others have suggested that the canned food was also infected with botulism, which causes acute food poisoning. Symptoms of lead poisoning include muscle weakness, reduced coordination and memory and concentration problems, as well as erratic and neurotic behaviour.

This could explain the bizarre behaviour of Franklin's remaining men, already weak from lack of food and scurvy, trying to drag a boat and sled loaded with silver spoons, books and cooking ovens—and weighing over 1,000 pounds—in a race to reach food before they starved to death.

CHAPTER

6

Roald Amundsen
(1872–1928)

EVEN AFTER THE NORTHWEST PASSAGE had finally been
found, the difficulties of navigating through shifting ice
packs, dense fog and howling blizzards, with the chance
of having to spend winters frozen into the ice, discounted
it as a shorter and easier route to the Orient and the Spice
Islands. Although it seems odd that no patriotic sailor set
out to traverse the passage, discovery for discovery's sake
had become passé. The new watchword was scientific exploration. However, there was one young man who dreamed of
sailing the Northwest Passage.

Roald Engelbregt Gravning Amundsen was born in
Norway on July 16, 1872—the youngest of four sons. His
father was a sea captain with his own fleet of sailing ships.

His mother wanted him to study medicine. When Amundsen completed school at the age of 18, he studied human anatomy by day, but by night he slept with his windows open to the frigid winter air to condition his body and dreamed of exploring the North and South poles. When his mother died in 1893, he sold his medical books and tried to talk his way onto the crew of various voyages heading north. The voyage leaders were not interested. They needed people with more qualifications than mere enthusiasm. In the meantime, Amundsen was devouring accounts of other explorers, such as Eivand Astrup, who travelled to the Arctic with Robert Peary, Fridtjof Nansen and Robert Falcon Scott. He realized that if he were a qualified sea captain, he would be able to take complete charge of his own expeditions, so he signed on with a sealing ship.

In 1896, the 24-year-old Amundsen joined the *Belgica* on an expedition to explore the Antarctic coast. Like many of his countrymen, Amundsen was accomplished at travelling on cross-country skis. He trained hard to keep his lean, muscular and over six-foot-tall body exceptionally fit. With his experience sailing in cold climates, he was now more qualified to join an exploration crew. Amundsen knew the experience would be invaluable and eagerly joined the *Belgica* as first mate, without pay.

The ship left Antwerp on August 16, 1897, and the following January the crew began charting islands along Gerlache Strait (named after the captain of the *Belgica*). The plan was that at the end of the Antarctic summer the crew would settle the captain, Dr. Frederick Cook and another man onshore with enough supplies to last the winter and then take the *Belgica* on to Australia. Instead, their ship became caught in the ice pack on the last day of February, and they were forced to drift in the ice all winter. The members of the crew, who were Russian, Belgian, Polish and Romanian, could not understand each other. They were cooped up on the ship with little to do and a shortage of food (all canned). In mid-May, the sun disappeared below the horizon for almost 10 weeks and layers of ice turned the ship's decks and rigging white.

The men began to show symptoms of scurvy. Dr. Cook made sure the men ate seal meat and penguin on a regular basis, even though he openly admitted that penguin tasted like smelly codfish, beef and duck cooked together in cod-liver oil and blood. He also used light therapy for those suffering from a lack of sunlight, sitting the men in front of an open fire. Even so, some of the men were convinced they were doomed to drift until they died. Two of them went mad. One simply climbed off the ship onto the ice and said he was going home to Belgium.

When spring finally arrived, work parties spent several weeks sawing and blasting their way free of the ice. Amundsen, who stayed reasonably healthy throughout the voyage, had observed and noted everything and spent many hours exhausting Dr. Cook's store of useful knowledge.

With what he had learned aboard the *Belgica* and from the accounts of Franklin's expeditions, which he had read with great interest, he could have written a lengthy and informed account of the pitfalls of polar exploration. Instead, he signed on to the *Oscar*, a family ship, and began to study for his master's certificate.

By 1900, Amundsen was 27 and chafing to lead his own expedition. The Northwest Passage beckoned; however, polar expeditions needed substantial financing. He needed sponsors, and the way to attract them was with the hope of some important scientific discovery. He decided to search for the current location of the north magnetic pole.

During the 15th century, it had become clear that compasses did not point to the fixed position of the North Pole, but deviated slightly from true north. Mapping this deviation became important for mariners. If they didn't allow for it in their calculations, they would not reach the destination they had marked on their charts. Later, during the 17th century, it also appeared that this deviation changed slightly from year to year. James Clark Ross had plotted the north magnetic pole's location from King William Island in 1831. Amundsen wanted to study its fluctuations and find out where it was in the early 1900s. He spent six weeks at the Hamburg Maritime Institute in Germany studying how to make accurate magnetic observations and then searched for a suitable ship.

The *Gjøa* was a 69-by-21-foot fishing sloop with a

shallow seven-and-a-half-foot draft. Critics claimed that she was too small, too old and too frail to survive Arctic waters. Amundsen countered that he didn't intend to force his way through the passage, as others had tried to do in ships that required twice the depth of water beneath them. Instead, he would use this small, agile vessel to finesse his way through. He took her on some test runs between Norway and Greenland, then reinforced her hull with three-inch oak planks and added iron strapping to her bow. He also installed a 13-horsepower diesel engine. When he was ready, he hired six sailors, one of whom had also been trained in magnetic observation. They stowed supplies and provisions carefully. Amundsen planned to travel light. They would catch their own fresh meat, and because hauling sleds used too much energy when the body was already fighting to keep warm, they would use dogs to pull their sleds. The expedition was about to depart when a crisis hit.

Amundsen had used all his money to buy the *Gjøa*. Money raised from sponsors had gone on essential equipment, and he had bought the rest of his supplies with promissory notes. Now, the possessor of one of those notes was having second thoughts, possibly because he was afraid that Amundsen, like so many others before him, would never return from this northern voyage. The merchant marched up to Amundsen and demanded payment within 24 hours. If he didn't get it, he said, stabbing his finger toward the *Gjøa*, he would seize the ship. Amundsen gathered his crew on board and, under the cover of darkness, cast off his lines and slipped out of the harbour. The night of June 16, 1903, was a miserable one with winds and heavy rain, but aboard the *Gjøa* the usually taciturn and solemn Amundsen was in good humour. As he passed celebratory tots of rum to his crew, his hooded, pale blue eyes sparkled in his lean, lined face with its drooping moustache and goatee. Finally, he was on his way.

Into the Northwest Passage

During his year aboard the *Belgica*, the quiet and sensitive Amundsen had seen the importance of good morale; therefore, he had chosen his crew well. Each man knew his area of responsibility and did what needed to be done. They travelled north along Davis Strait, stopping in at Godhavn, Greenland, to buy dog teams and at Dalrymple Rock for supplies. From there they headed east through Lancaster Sound and stopped at Beechey Island to pay tribute to Franklin and his men, who had spent their first winter there (1845–1846), and to visit the graves of the Franklin expedition's first three casualties.

With mixed feelings they continued into unknown waters, travelling south along Peel Sound. So far, the voyage had been relatively uneventful and their way clear of ice, but in Franklin Strait, the *Gjøa* ran into underwater rocks. The men managed to work her free, but that evening a fire broke out in the engine room. Earlier that day, one of the men had noticed a leaking gas tank in the engine room. Amundsen ordered that the gasoline be transferred to a spare tank. If this had not been done promptly, the entire ship could have gone up in flames. As it was, the fire was quickly extinguished with only minor damage to the ship.

The *Gjøa* grounded again on a reef off Matty Island at high tide three days later. The men threw heavy cases of dog food overboard and moved the rest of their load to one side so the *Gjøa* would heel. They put out a small anchor to make her heel further and waited for the next high tide. It peaked that evening, but despite all their efforts, they couldn't move her. By morning, a gale had blown in, and the men tried pulling on the small anchor again and again. The ship shuddered and groaned but stayed put. There was one last thing they could try. They raised the sails, which filled with wind and lifted the *Gjøa*, sending her banging and grinding across the reef. Each time the waves sucked back she settled onto the rocks, her sails taut and her mast ready to snap at any moment. She was being driven to the edge of the reef, but the rocks were higher there, the water over the reef even shallower. The men laboured to drop more cases of provisions overboard, expecting their little herring boat to break up at any moment. They held on through one final juddering slide, and she was floating freely again. The crew rushed to check for leaks while Amundsen made for the crow's nest to direct the helmsman around the shoals. The helmsman shouted that she wouldn't steer. She pitched over another large wave. As she slapped down into the trough, her rudder was knocked back into place and her steering was restored. Amundsen's prayer had been answered. The *Gjøa* was still intact. From then on, whenever they sailed in unfamiliar waters Amundsen kept one man on the prow and one in the crow's nest to watch for rocks.

They motored south along Rae Strait. On September 9, they spotted a small, sheltered harbour along the southeast shore of King William Island. This was close enough to the north magnetic pole for precise measurements to be made. While it must have been hard for Amundsen to pull into the harbour instead of continuing west through the passage, he realized the importance of honouring his agreement with his sponsors. They anchored the *Gjøa* close to the beach and used packing crates to build huts and an observatory on the shores of what became known as Gjøa Havn. The crates had been specially built with copper nails instead of the usual iron nails that would interfere with magnetic readings. They set up their equipment and began to record fluctuations in the earth's magnetism.

Finding the North Magnetic Pole

The crew began to lay up a store of meat. Amundsen preferred live animals to dead ones so was not much of a hunter. Instead, he made himself useful transporting carcasses to the ship by sled and discovered that driving a dog team was not as easy as it looked. He found the whole thing highly frustrating until a group of Inuit came by and gave him lessons. They were the first of numerous visitors, and Amundsen, fascinated by the way they lived in such an inhospitable climate, learned all he could from them. Concerned that the Inuit, who greatly outnumbered them, might decide to attack them and steal their belongings, Amundsen staged the blowing up of an empty snow-block house with a wave of his hand. He also ordered his crew members to steer clear of the Inuit women, whose cultural practice was to share their favours with visitors.

In March 1904, Amundsen made his first attempt to reach the north magnetic pole. He failed but learned from his mistakes. On his third attempt, he and Peder Ristvedt, travelling on skis with a dog team hauling their supplies, reached Cape Adelaide on Boothia Peninsula, where Ross had measured the magnetic pole in 1831. Their instruments indicated that it had moved some 40 miles to the northeast. Wanting to pinpoint the location exactly, the two men travelled on, but they soon had only enough food left for their return journey. Amundsen's success as an explorer lay in the fact that he always planned meticulously and never took uncalculated risks. He therefore decided that they should return to Gjøa Havn and leave the north magnetic pole for another trip. Over the following year, crew members, in teams of two, continued to explore nearby coastlines and islands, but Amundsen, wanting to be fair and give the other men opportunities to explore, never did reach the new magnetic pole, something he later regretted. However, he proved that the magnetic pole did move, determined its approximate new location and collected valuable information on magnetic fluctuation.

A Journey Resumed

As summer arrived and the ice melted, the men dismantled their camp and loaded their belongings back aboard the *Gjøa*. They left Gjøa Havn on August 13, 1905, and inched westwards through the narrow Simpson Strait. The lead line flew up and down as the sailors checked the scant inches of water below their keel, and the lookouts waved their arms first to port then to starboard, pointing the *Gjøa* around rocks and shallows as she rounded the southern end of King William Island. Thankful for his ship's shallow draft, Amundsen was immensely relieved when the water grew deeper again. They continued west along Queen Maud and Coronation gulfs, now in waters that had been sailed before.

Amundsen was sleeping in his cabin on the morning of August 26 when he was woken by shouts. He rushed out onto the deck to see what was wrong. His second-in-command was shouting, "Vessel in sight!" Approaching them was a whaling ship that had come from the Pacific. There was no doubt now that they had come through the Northwest Passage. Amundsen felt a strange tightness in his throat and blinked away tears as he realized that he had fulfilled his boyhood dream. The captain of the whaler, the

Charles Hanson of San Francisco, was thrilled to be the first to make contact with Amundsen after his historic voyage. Not only had he sailed the Northwest Passage, but he had also sailed through Rae Strait, proving that John Rae had indeed found the missing section between King William Island and Boothia Peninsula. However, the *Gjøa*'s journey was not yet over. Amundsen's emotional high quickly turned to frustration as he found their way blocked by ice off Herschel Island along the Yukon coast. The crew had little choice but to settle in for another Arctic winter.

Stymied

A British newspaper, the *Times*, had agreed to pay well for Amundsen's exclusive story, but the nearest telegraph office was in Fort Egbert, outside Eagle City, Alaska. Amundsen, worried that his success might somehow be leaked to other newspapers, set out alone for Eagle City by ski and dogsled. Some 500 miles later, in the telegraph office on December 5, 1905, he cabled a long report to the *Times*. Unfortunately for Amundsen, the telegraph office was along the United States Army's telegraph line to Alaska. His story was leaked to American newspapers, and the *Times*, outscooped, refused to pay for his stale news. Amundsen stayed in Eagle City long enough to collect mail from home and arrived back at the *Gjøa* on March 12, 1906. More bad news awaited him. One of his crew was seriously ill and died a few days later.

By July, the men were able to start working their

ship through the ice. They reached Nome, Alaska, on August 31, 1906, and after a great celebration sailed on to San Francisco. The *Gjøa* remained on display in Golden Gate Park until 1974, when she was sent to her final resting place at the Norsk Sjøfartsmuseum in Oslo.

Amundsen's next goal was to be first to the North Pole, but in September 1909, Robert Peary announced that he'd reached it in April of that year. Peary didn't know that Frederick Cook had just claimed to have reached the North Pole in 1908. Amundsen then aimed to reach the South Pole and, keeping his plans secret, beat Robert Falcon Scott by 35 days. Scott's attempt was ill-prepared and badly planned, and his party perished from starvation, frostbite, scurvy and dehydration on their retreat back to their ship.

Next, Amundsen decided to repeat Fridtjof Nansen's attempt to drift over the North Pole in a boat frozen into the ice pack. He spent two winters in the *Maud* frozen into coastal ice and another three along the continental shelf off northeastern Siberia before giving up. His attempt to fly over the North Pole in an airplane failed, too. Later, in May 1926, he flew over the North Pole with two other men in a hydrogen-filled airship, the *Norge*.

Later, in a strange twist of fate, doubts were cast over the previous North Pole claims (Cook in 1908, Peary in 1909 and Byrd in 1926, just a few days before Amundsen's *Norge* flight), and it is entirely possible that Roald Amundsen, Lincoln Ellsworth and Umberto Nobile were the first to reach the North Pole after all. Their route across unknown territory showed that there were no land masses below. The final puzzle piece of the world was slotted into place.

When Nobile's new airship crashed in the Arctic in May 1928, Amundsen joined the rescue party. He took off in a seaplane for Spitsbergen on June 18, 1928. Three hours after takeoff, the plane stopped transmitting signals and disappeared. Nobile and his crew were rescued on June 22, but Amundsen was not so lucky. Searchers found a wing float and a fuel tank that had been modified, possibly to make a raft, but no sign of any passengers or crew. In August and September 2009, a team of experts assembled on two Norwegian vessels to search the Arctic Ocean in the vicinity of Bear Island for the wreckage of Amundsen's plane. The search was unsuccessful.

7

Henry Larsen
(1899–1964)

ALTHOUGH ROALD AMUNDSEN HAD SQUEAKED through the Northwest Passage in the compact *Gjøa*, his route was very shallow in places and would not accommodate larger commercial ships. Interest in the passage waned, and explorers moved on to other goals. After Britain transferred the rest of her Arctic possessions to Canada in 1880, however, other countries, including Norway and the United States, began to question Canada's sovereignty.

The Americans established a whaling post on Herschel Island, and with the gold rush, more Americans came pouring into the Yukon. The Canadian government realized it would have to protect Canada's interests. It sent in the Royal Canadian Mounted Police (RCMP) to set up permanent posts from which they could send out patrols and establish a national presence. At first, the RCMP relied on civilian trading ships for transportation and supplies, but this was not convenient; after several years, the RCMP commissioned their own supply ship, the *St. Roch*.

Larsen and the *St. Roch*

The *St. Roch* was launched on May 7, 1928, but staffing her created another problem. While the RCMP attracted skilled horsemen, it had a severe shortage of competent sailors. Of the eight men chosen to sail on the *St. Roch*'s maiden voyage, five had never been to sea before. Of the other three, one had served in the British Navy, one had served in the merchant marine and the third was Henry Asbjørn Larsen.

Larsen was born in Norway on September 30, 1899. His favourite subjects in school were history and geography, and he was familiar with the expeditions of Frobisher and Franklin, as well as national heroes such as Vilhjalmur Stefansson, Fridtjof Nansen and Roald Amundsen. At the age of 15, Larsen went to sea. Working a sailing ship meant long hours and mediocre food. Nevertheless, by February 1919, Larsen had made several round trips to South America. He signed up on a steamer that had no rigging to climb, better food and enough fresh water to wash in, but he missed the camaraderie of sailing ships. Upon his return to Oslo, he attended the Norwegian State Navigation School and then completed his compulsory military service in the

Norwegian Navy. When he was 23, Larsen embarked on what looked like the beginning of a promising career with a shipping line. But then he met Oscar Omdahl.

Omdahl had been Amundsen's pilot on the *Maud* and, having finally abandoned her in the ice near Wrangel Island, was on his way back to Oslo. Larsen found room for some of Omdahl's luggage in his cabin and asked the pilot about his adventures. By the time they reached Oslo, Larsen was longing to travel through the Arctic. The shipping line promoted Larsen to third mate, but he realized that he had to follow his heart and left to look for work on a ship that sailed Arctic waters.

Only one HBC ship and a couple of others from San Francisco sailed to the Arctic. Larsen tried to contact the owners, but without success. Then he read a newspaper article about a man named Christian Klengenberg from Coronation Gulf, who was in Seattle preparing his schooner to sail to the Arctic with supplies for his family and a number of goods for trade. Taking a chance, Larsen left Vancouver for Seattle. The *Maid of Orleans* was tied up along the waterfront, and Klengenberg and his two sons were aboard. What's more, they needed a navigator and hired Larsen immediately as the captain's mate. He set to work getting the ship ready. At the end of June 1927, the fully loaded *Maid of Orleans* pulled out of Seattle.

Their first stop was the RCMP District Headquarters on Herschel Island, where Corporal Pasley joined them with his sled, sled dogs and dog food. By the time they dropped Pasley off at Baillie Island, he and Larsen had become friends.

Klengenberg and his sons had been away for 18 months, and when they pulled into their home harbour at Rymer Point on Victoria Island, the 150 inhabitants greeted them enthusiastically. They unloaded supplies and then left to take care of some other errands. Unfortunately, their ship came up against heavy ice and they were forced to spend the winter at Herschel Island. Here, Larsen spent more time with the RCMP officers. He liked the men and envied their way of life. One day, he confided that he would like to join the RCMP and work in the North. His confidant replied that he would need Canadian citizenship first, which he could apply for after he'd lived in Canada for four years. The RCMP officer told Larsen that he seemed to be the kind of person they needed. He also told him that they were hoping to have an Arctic supply ship of their own soon. Larsen wanted to work on this RCMP ship and chafed impatiently at the wait to apply for citizenship.

When spring came, they sailed back to Victoria Island and then returned to Seattle in September 1925. Larsen was not paid for the months spent at Herschel Island, but his experiences were worth more to him than money. He filled the next couple of years with a steamer trip to the tropics and a job repairing roads, which he hated. When he had spent his requisite four years in Canada, he applied for citizenship.

On November 18, 1927, Larsen swore his allegiance to his new country. At about the same time came the news that the RCMP were going to begin building a ship the following year. Larsen's friend, Corporal Pasley, was in charge and wanted Larsen on his crew. At the beginning of 1928, Larsen applied to join the RCMP and was soon undergoing training.

Like Amundsen's ship *Maud*, the *St. Roch* was specially designed to withstand the pressure of ice. Her hull was egg-shaped, so that instead of being held and squeezed by ice, she would pop out of it. The *St. Roch* was reinforced with thick planks of ironwood, an Australian gumwood that would withstand the grinding of ice. Her beams were thick, to prevent the hold from being crushed, and her rudder could be lifted up to protect it from ice and rocks. Nevertheless, she had numerous shortcomings in design and was the most uncomfortable ship that Larsen had ever been on. There was always a bolt where someone wanted to rest his head, or something for a sailor to stub his toes on. The compass was in the wheelhouse, where the helmsman could barely see over the bow of the ship to take bearings. Larsen thought it a good thing that her sailors were all policemen used to taking orders, because experienced sailors would never have wanted to work aboard such a ship.

The skipper and engineer were provided by the shipbuilders to put the ship through her paces as far as Herschel Island where, if there were no problems, they were to leave the RCMP officers in charge. At the last minute, Corporal Pasley withdrew because his wife was not allowed to accompany him. Larsen was immediately promoted to mate.

They sailed from Vancouver on June 28, 1928. The egg-shaped hull rocked easily in the wind, and the Mounties from the prairies became seasick when the first gale hit them. After five days, however, their seasickness left for good. Larsen was a true sailor who always looked for opportunities to raise the sails. His crew had to do all the hard work involved, and they thought that any nominal increase in speed wasn't worth it. They didn't enjoy working the lead line either. Although it weighed only eight pounds, it began to feel a lot heavier after a couple of hours of throwing it out in front of the ship and hauling it back in. It didn't help that the operator had to have bare hands to feel the fathom markers along the rope. The ice chafed and cracked his skin, which in turn left his hands stinging from the salt water.

They made a number of stops as they travelled north. In Teller, north of Nome, Alaska, they saw the remains of Amundsen's airship. Larsen also noticed some of the locals wearing parkas made from its silk. When the shipbuilders' skipper and engineer left the ship, Larsen was surprised, but pleased, to be placed in charge of the ship. Sergeant Anderton, an officious man, was placed in charge of police matters, but Larsen, with his easygoing nature, managed to make the arrangement work.

The officers aboard the *St. Roch* were kept busy. They patrolled western Arctic waters acting as a floating detachment that kept law and order and took care of government tasks such as collecting customs duties and taxes, selling hunting licences and making welfare and pension payments. The RCMP officers also delivered supplies to other detachments, as well as patients to the hospital and children to the school in Aklavik. They delivered mail, gathered vital population statistics and explored new shipping routes. The group spent their first winter in Langton Bay. None of the other men had overwintered on a ship before, and Larsen was grateful for all Klengenberg had taught him. They built a frame over the deck and covered it with canvas to make room for a workshop and a space where they could pace around when they couldn't leave the ship. They cut hundreds of ice blocks from a nearby lake to provide drinking water through the winter and placed snow blocks around the ship for insulation to help keep them warm.

The ship had numerous visitors, and the cook could always find something to ease a toothache or a cough. He also handed out laxatives, as the Inuit diet made them prone to constipation. The locals were good hunters, and there weren't any crimes or fights to deal with. Larsen and another officer went on short sled trips to visit nearby communities. They tried coating the sled runners with thick oatmeal, instead of the mud the Inuit used. It worked well with a thin coat of ice over the top and doubled as an emergency food supply. Larsen also found out that kindness and encouragement worked on the sled dogs in much the same way it worked on people. When the dogs were getting tired toward the end of a long run, he would sing to them to keep their spirits up. In the evenings, aboard their stationary ship, the RCMP officers read or cut and sewed skins and hides into socks and boots while listening to one of their two skilled storytellers. In May, Larsen received a wireless message telling him that he had been promoted to the rank of corporal. Seven weeks later, after seven months in Langton Bay, the *St. Roch* was released from the thawing ice and the detachment headed back to Herschel Island.

By 1935, Larsen was a sergeant, and on February 7 he married Mary Hargreaves. Wives were still not allowed to accompany their husbands, so Mary lived in Vancouver and Larsen joined her when he was on leave. While he regretted being away when a daughter and then a son were born, he loved his work and didn't want to give up his dream of sailing the Northwest Passage. When Commissioner Sir James MacBrien visited the officers aboard the *St. Roch*, Larsen suggested that they might proceed east through the Northwest Passage after their stay on King William Island, which was scheduled for the winter of 1936–1937. The commissioner was in favour of this but pointed out that duties had to come first. It wasn't until the Second World War broke out that Larsen was finally given his chance.

Passage from West to East
The *St. Roch* was one of the few ships not requisitioned for war duty. She was too slow. However, the Canadian government

was worried about enemy activity in the Arctic. Hitler had occupied Denmark, leaving Greenland vulnerable. Allied aircraft production was heavily dependent on a mineral called cryolite, which was mined in Greenland, and the government wanted to secure the mine. Larsen was asked to deliver supplies to the various RCMP detachments and then continue east to Halifax, watching for signs of unusual activity. He was also asked to keep his assignment a secret. This created a problem because the *St. Roch* needed an extra engine to charge the electric light batteries, as well as a new sharp metal sheath around her bow to help cut through the ice. However, the naval dockyard at Esquimalt had more work than it could handle, and fixing up the *St. Roch* was not given top priority because her real mission was not generally known. Larsen did what he could to move his ship to the top of the work list and was finally ready to sail on June 21, 1940. The two old hands on board and a few enthusiastic newcomers all thought they were on a routine supply trip. When they reached Alaska, Larsen revealed that he was going to navigate the Northwest Passage and asked if any of them wanted to leave the ship. None of them did, which was just as well, as they would have been stranded in Alaska. When they ran into ice they were forced to find a winter berth in Walker Bay on the east coast of Victoria Island. Larsen was disappointed. He had hoped to make history by sailing the passage in one season. Instead, the officers took advantage of the opportunity to patrol the surrounding area and look for signs of illegal trapping. For

Christmas dinner, they ate the Arctic owls the Inuit called *ukpiks*, and Larsen listened to radio messages from his wife and daughter.

The spring brought further disappointment in the form of orders to sail for Tuktoyaktuk to help deliver supplies. It was here that one of the original crew members, Officer Chartrand, collapsed briefly, but after a couple of days of rest he seemed fine. They departed, sailing east again, and pressed on through hail and snow, hoping they had time to reach Halifax before winter caught up to them. They were approaching Matty Island, where Amundsen had almost lost the *Gjøa*, when Larsen saw a solid ice pack blocking their way ahead. He turned against the strong current and steered for a tiny islet off Boothia Peninsula. As a snowstorm blew up, the crew dropped two anchors and spent the night trying to gauge whether or not the anchors were holding, as chunks of ice crashed against the hull. They kept the engine running in case they had to make a fast escape. In the morning, the wind changed and ice crashed in from the north instead of northeast. The men passed another sleepless night. Some of them wanted to make for Gjøa Havn and settle in for the winter, but Larsen didn't think this was a good idea, given the weather conditions. As he was loath to turn west again, he carefully studied an old Admiralty chart. It showed an inlet in Pasley Bay that would offer them protection. However, he knew that the chart was 85 years old. Larsen raised the anchors and prayed that the inlet would be where it was supposed to be.

To his immense relief it was. They anchored again but were soon being swept along with their anchors dragging through icy slush. They winched them in as the wind blasted particles of ice into their faces, freezing their eyelashes together. In the early hours of the morning, the *St. Roch* was pushed against a shoal, her port and starboard anchors dragging again. After spinning around, her port rail dug down into the ice while the starboard side of her hull tilted to the sky. The men instinctively hung on to anything they could reach to keep themselves on board, despite the fact that freezing to death in the water would likely be a faster and easier death than being slowly crushed with their ship. When it seemed that their situation was completely hopeless, another huge chunk of ice hit and knocked the *St. Roch* back into deep water. The ship began to right herself; but now she was being carried parallel to the shore, kept from being pushed in and grounded only by the ice packed along the bay. Larsen saw a large rock up ahead. He ran to unwind a wire cable attached to the deck in front of the foremast and yelled at three of his men to take the end, climb down onto the ice and wind the cable around the rock. They just had time to secure the cable before it snapped tight, holding their ship in place. As if at some signal, the wind suddenly died and everything settled into a surreal calm. The men were exhausted, but they secured their hardy little ship with lines to the shore before falling into their bunks for some much-needed rest.

By morning, the bay was a solid mass of ice, glittering blue

The RCMP ship *St. Roch*, frozen into the ice in Pasley Bay, Boothia Inlet, during the winter of 1941–42. GLENBOW ARCHIVES NA-1344-8

in the sunshine. Although they were disappointed at being kept from their goal, it was as good a place as any to spend the winter. They sent out word of their location by radio and began another season of sled patrols and census taking.

On February 13, Officer Chartrand collapsed with pains around his stomach and heart; minutes later he died. Despite the constantly rough conditions in which they lived, there had not been one serious accident. This was the first loss aboard the *St. Roch* during her 14 years afloat. Larsen and the other men were shocked. They notified RCMP headquarters, who relayed that his family wanted him to have a proper Roman Catholic burial. However, no aircraft could fly in or out during winter, so Larsen and Constable

Hunt went to fetch the nearest Catholic priest from Pelly Bay, some 400 miles away. While the others built a coffin and stored Chartrand's body in a nearby snowbank, Hunt and Larsen packed two months' provisions onto the dogsleds. They left on February 24 and reached Father Henri's mission on March 31. The priest was surprised to see them but said he would make the trip in May. They stayed for six days, attending the Easter services, and arrived back at the *St. Roch* on May 6. Father Henri arrived two weeks later. He conducted a Requiem Mass on deck, and they buried Chartrand on a nearby hill. They covered the shallow grave with rocks, so that animals would not disturb it, and marked it with a 15-foot cairn and a cross with an engraved nameplate.

Miraculously, their ship had not been seriously damaged during her violent arrival in Pasley Bay, and at the beginning of August 1942 they were able to work their way out, leaving Chartrand behind. They hadn't gone far when a lump of ice hooked itself under the keel and jammed the rudder. Worried about rudder and propeller damage, the men tried to chop the ice away but couldn't free the ship. They prepared the lifeboats with spare clothes and provisions so that they could grab them at a moment's notice if the ship began to sink. A few days later, the wind did what the men had been unable to do, springing the *St. Roch* off the melting lump into clear water. Again, she was undamaged, but ahead they could see only more ice. They sat for two weeks being carried slowly southward to the place where the *Erebus* and the *Terror* had become permanently trapped. When they saw a lead in the ice ahead, they started up the *St. Roch*'s engine only to find that one of her cylinders had cracked. The engineers managed to bypass the damaged cylinder so the engine would run, albeit with less power. Their chances of reaching Halifax before winter were getting slimmer. Some days their progress was limited to a few nautical miles, but the men tried to stay cheerful.

Then one night, a gale blew down Franklin Strait and opened up the ice as far as they could see. Larsen, with his outstanding ability to read the ice, worked their ship through the leads to Bellot Strait where, thinking to cut some distance off their route, he headed into the strait. The tide and current gave them extra speed. They were making good progress when they noticed a solid white line across the water in front of them. Larsen slowed the engine and made out an iceberg grounded on some shallows. The current and tide were pushing thousands of pounds of ice against the iceberg, and their ship was heading straight toward it. Larsen cranked up the engine and spun the wheel to swerve away from the iceberg. The ship groaned as ice piled up around them in whirlpools caused by meeting tides. After almost an hour, the changing current weakened her hold and the ship broke free. Her thankful crew made their way out of the strait and pressed on through unfamiliar waters.

A few days later, they anchored in Pond Inlet, where the

entire population greeted them. They had come through the Northwest Passage with no sightings of enemy activity, but still had to reach Halifax. They unpacked the Arctic gear they would no longer need, along with their dogs, which howled piteously when they saw their home and masters leaving without them. Larsen turned the *St. Roch* south into Davis Strait and continued along the coast of Baffin Island and Labrador, unable to see much at all. When he sighted a fishing boat, they followed her into Bateau Harbour. While in Newfoundland, the ship's cracked cylinder was repaired, and her crew received an enthusiastic reception from the locals before being ordered to proceed with one of the convoys that was headed for Halifax.

Even with the engine fixed, they were unable to keep up against stiff headwinds. Larsen raised his sails and hoped that any enemy submarines in the area would not be interested in a small sailing ship. When they approached Sydney Harbour on Cape Breton Island, a naval patrol officer asked them to identify themselves. Larsen said that they were on the vessel *St. Roch* from Vancouver bound for Halifax. The officer replied that they were in Sydney, a long way off course. Larsen countered that he was not off course at all, because they had sailed the northern route. The officer had difficulty believing that the bedraggled men in the battered sailing ship were RCMP officers who had just sailed the Northwest Passage, but he eventually allowed them to spend the night in the harbour. They reached Halifax the next day, October 11, 1942. They should have been jubilant, but they were all exhausted. They were also overwhelmed by the busy harbour after years in the Arctic.

They were greeted and congratulated by a few of the local RCMP officers. Some members of the crew were transferred immediately to other postings, while those who remained tried to summon enough energy to tidy up the ship. Larsen had reports to write that included all the navigational data he had collected, as well as information on the living conditions among the Inuit. After reporting to the RCMP commissioner in Ottawa, he was finally given a few weeks' leave. Larsen was promoted to staff sergeant, and each member of the voyage, including Chartrand, was awarded the Polar Medal by King George VI. Only after he was rested and given time to reflect could Larsen celebrate the fact that he was the second man ever to negotiate the Northwest Passage and the first to tackle it from west to east.

A Journey through Time

In the summer of 1944, Larsen was given another opportunity to sail the Northwest Passage in one season. He chose the northern route along Lancaster Sound, Melville Sound and Prince of Wales Strait because these waters were deeper and would provide access for larger commercial ships. It was a journey through time as he and his men stopped off to see Franklin's memorial on Beechey Island and other relics, cairns and memorials that told the history of the infamous passage. Although they still encountered ice and fog, the westward journey to Vancouver was less perilous than their earlier route eastward. It took only 86 days, and they arrived in Vancouver on October 16, 1944. The *St. Roch* was the first ship to sail the Northwest Passage in one season and the first to sail it in both directions.

Larsen and the *St. Roch* Retire

Larsen sailed the *St. Roch* to the Arctic two more times, but the Arctic was changing. He was now able to fly home from Aklavik for Christmas, and with communities becoming established and accessible by aircraft, the RCMP no longer needed a floating detachment. During the final two voyages, Larsen said goodbye to his many friends in the Arctic, where he had become known as "Henry with the Big Ship." Appropriately, he spent his last winter on Herschel Island, where his round of Arctic duties had begun.

Moved to an office onshore, he was placed in command of a division that covered the Northwest and Yukon Territories along with remote parts of Quebec and Ontario. Having travelled extensively through the Arctic, he was aware of the problems. He tried to prepare for the changing role of the RCMP in the North and worried about the consequences of the Inuit trying to assimilate a foreign culture in a relatively brief time period. In 1953, a new Department of Northern Affairs and National Resources began to take over Arctic administration.

St. Roch's uniquely shaped hull and slow speed made her unsuitable for service outside the Arctic, but in 1950, Larsen sent her to Halifax through the Panama Canal, making her the first ship to circumnavigate North America. From Halifax, she spent several months carrying supplies to RCMP detachments in Newfoundland and Labrador. When she was no longer needed, the RCMP sold her to the city of Vancouver, and in July 1954, Larsen sailed her back through the Panama Canal. He arrived in Vancouver in October and was given a tremendous welcome. It must have warmed his heart after the low-key welcomes that met both of his Northwest Passage triumphs. When the ceremonies were over, it took the city some time to decide what to do with the awkward little ship that Larsen had grown to love, but with the government's help she was winched ashore, and in 1958 the Vancouver Maritime Museum was built around her. In 1962, she was declared a National Historic Site. In 1971, she was restored to her original 1944 appearance.

In 1960, Larsen was awarded the Royal Canadian Geographical Society's first Massey Medal for his outstanding contribution to Canadian geographical knowledge and in recognition of the first west-to-east voyage through the Northwest Passage. In 1961, Superintendent Larsen retired from the RCMP. He died on October 29, 1964, and his ashes were buried in the RCMP national cemetery in Regina.

Epilogue

WHILE FRANKLIN HAS BEEN CREDITED with finding the Northwest Passage, it was really an accumulation of knowledge from many explorers, some of them searching for Franklin, that led to its ultimate discovery. With masterful Arctic sailing skills, guts, determination and their specially adapted ships, Amundsen and Larsen were eventually able to fulfill the dreams of all those who had searched before them. There isn't room in this book to mention all of the explorers who found their way to the maze of channels and straits that make up the Northwest Passage, but their legacies remain in the names on the maps and charts of the Arctic.

Although these explorers answered many questions,

some also left mysteries behind. Why did Henry Hudson sail up and down James Bay as though he was conducting a systematic survey? In his article "Into the Great Bay," Carl Schuster suggests that he was looking for a safe harbour from which to explore the mineral wealth of the Canadian Shield. It's also possible that Hudson had finally lost his grip on reality.

The mysteries around the Franklin expedition are harder to explain away. Why have Franklin's grave, his journals and the expedition records never been found? There should have been two sets of expedition records, one from each ship. Henry Larsen hoped to find them and was convinced that one day someone would. However, in his book *The Franklin Conspiracy*, Jeffrey Blair Latta suggests that the British Admiralty suppressed or destroyed them because they were keeping something secret. To date, these mysteries remain unsolved, as do the challenges to Canadian sovereignty over the Arctic islands and waterways.

When Britain transferred her remaining Arctic possessions to Canada in 1880, she included all islands adjacent to any such territories. Reasons for other countries to challenge Canada's sovereignty and boundaries are becoming more numerous as time goes on. Some of the islands were discovered by explorers of other nationalities, including Norwegian Otto Sverdrup, who was the first person known to set foot on Axel Heiberg, Ellef Ringnes and Amund Ringnes Islands (between 1898 and 1902). Rights to fishing grounds and mineral resources are at stake, and the route between Asia and Europe through the Northwest Passage is 4,700 nautical miles shorter than the route through the Panama Canal. There is debate over whether polar ice is contracting permanently or merely seasonally, but ongoing improvements in technology have made the Northwest Passage more navigable in recent years.

In 1903, the Canadian government realized that claims supported by occupation and administration were more likely to be approved in international law. They began to establish RCMP posts and to patrol the Arctic waterways. However, large areas remained uninhabited and virtually undefended, leading other countries, including the United States, to demand that these be governed as international waters. Determined to defend Canada's sovereignty, Prime Minister Stephen Harper has set in motion numerous exercises and initiatives to improve the health of indigenous communities in the North, assert Canada's presence and demonstrate its ability to defend the area.

Significant Dates

1492 Christopher Columbus sails from Spain, convinced he can reach the east by sailing west. He discovers Cuba, the Bahamas, Haiti and the Dominican Republic. Pope Alexander VI grants Spain sovereignty over the New World and Portugal sovereignty over Africa and the East.

1497 John Cabot sails from Bristol, England, looking for a new route to Cathay and the East. He finds Newfoundland and its rich fishing grounds.

1498 Cabot sails from England once again but disappears. Only one of his five ships returns to England.

1551 English merchants form the Muscovy Company to find a northeast passage to the East.

1554 Sir Hugh Willoughby and his crew die mysteriously and suddenly on board their ship while attempting to navigate the Northeast Passage to Cathay and India.

1576–78 Martin Frobisher sails on three voyages to look for a northeast or northwest passage but is sidetracked by the search for gold.

1588 Frobisher is knighted for his bravery during the defeat of the Spanish Armada.

1594 Frobisher is wounded while attacking the Spanish in France and dies from infection.

1607–9 Henry Hudson sails in three expeditions to search for a northeast passage.

1609 Italian astronomer and physicist Galileo Galilei improves on a new Dutch invention and begins building telescopes with a magnification power of eight or nine.

1610 Henry Hudson searches for a northwest passage but is cast adrift in a small boat by his starving crew, never to be seen again.

1675 The Royal Observatory is founded in England by King Charles II in order to find a way to measure longitude at sea.

1700 Shipbuilders begin to replace the tiller, attached to the rudder for steering, with a wheel.

1714 The British Parliament votes to award £20,000 to anyone who can devise an accurate way to measure longitude.

1736 English carpenter John Harrison (1693–1776) solves the longitude problem by building a clock that keeps accurate time aboard a damp, pitching sailboat.

1754 James Lind, a naval surgeon, proves that vitamin C prevents scurvy. It is 1795 before the Admiralty orders that lemon juice and, later, limes be supplied to British sailors.

1772 Samuel Hearne proves that there is no northwest passage leading out of Hudson Bay.

1775 James Cook makes history by returning from his second voyage around the world without losing a single sailor to scurvy. He uses an official copy of John Harrison's No. 4 timepiece to work out his precise longitude.

1778 On his third voyage, Cook sails north up the west coast of the United States in search of the Northwest Passage but is stopped by impenetrable ice. Not knowing that he has charted the Pacific entrance to the Northwest Passage, he returns to the Hawaiian Islands, where he is killed.

1822 John Franklin returns to England from a disastrous Arctic expedition.

Significant Dates

1825 Franklin leaves on a much more successful Arctic mapping expedition.

1845 Franklin sails down the Thames River on May 19, in charge of the biggest and best-provisioned expedition ever, to search for the final section of the Northwest Passage.

1847 Franklin dies of natural causes on June 11 on King William Island. The rest of his men slowly succumb to illness and starvation.

1854 John Rae is the first European to hear news of the lost Franklin expedition. He discovers the middle section of the Northwest Passage.

1884 Now that longitude can be measured, the prime meridian is located at Greenwich, England.

1890s The British government bans lead soldering on the inside of food cans.

1893 John Rae dies in London, England, and is buried in Kirkwall in the Orkneys.

1903 Roald Amundsen leaves Norway in the *Gjøa* on June 16 to locate the north magnetic pole and navigate the Northwest Passage.

1903 In order to protect Canada's interests in the North, the Canadian government begins to establish RCMP posts and to patrol Arctic waterways.

1906 Amundsen and his crew reach Nome, Alaska, on August 31 and celebrate their successful east-west traverse of the Northwest Passage.

1914 The Panama Canal opens to world commerce.

1928 On his way to search for a fellow explorer on June 18, Amundsen's plane crashes into the Arctic Ocean. His body is never found.

1942 Henry Larsen reaches Halifax after sailing the *St. Roch* through the Northwest Passage.

1944 Larsen arrives in Vancouver on October 16. His second journey through the Northwest Passage has taken 86 days.

Bibliography

Beattie, Owen and John Geiger. *Frozen In Time*. Vancouver: Douglas & McIntyre Ltd., 2004.

Berton, Pierre. *The Arctic Grail*. Toronto: McClelland and Stewart, 1988.

Borden, Louise. *Sea Clocks: The Story of Longitude*. New York: Margaret K. McElderry Books, 2004.

Brown, Warren. *The Search for the Northwest Passage*. New York: Chelsea House Publishers, 1991.

Cookman, Scott. *Ice Blink*. New York: John Wiley & Sons Inc., 2000.

Delgado, James P. *Across the Top of the World: The Quest for the Northwest Passage*. Vancouver: Douglas & McIntyre Ltd., 1999.

_____. *Arctic Workhorse: The RCMP Schooner St. Roch*. Victoria: TouchWood Editions Ltd., 2003.

Douglas, George M. *Lands Forlorn*. New York: G.P. Putnam's Sons, 1914.

Flaherty, Leo. *Roald Amundsen and the Quest for the South Pole*. New York: Chelsea House Publishers, 1992.

Franklin, John. *Journey to the Shores of the Polar Sea*. Vancouver: Douglas & McIntyre, 2000.

Gardiner, Juliet and Neil Wenborn. *The Companion to British History*. London: Collins & Brown Ltd., 1995.

Howarth, David. *British Sea Power*. London: Constable & Robinson Ltd., 1974.

Humble, Richard. *The Expeditions of Amundsen*. London: Franklin Watts Inc., 1991.

Bibliography

Johnson, Donald S. *Charting the Sea of Darkness: The Four Voyages of Henry Hudson*. Camden, ME: McGraw-Hill Inc., 1993.

Keay, John, ed. *The Mammoth Book of Explorers*. New York: Carroll & Graf Publishers, 2002.

Kenyon, W.A. *Tokens of Possession: The Northern Voyages of Martin Frobisher*. Toronto: University of Toronto Press, 1975.

Kimmel, Elizabeth Cody. *The Look It Up Book of Explorers*. New York: Random House Inc., 2004.

Larsen, Henry A. *The Big Ship*. Toronto: McClelland and Stewart Ltd., 1967.

Latta, Jeffrey Blair. *The Franklin Conspiracy*. Toronto: Hounslow Press, 2001.

Lehane, Brendan. *The Northwest Passage*. Alexandria, VA: Time-Life Books, 1981.

Lomask, Milton. *Great Lives*. New York: Charles Scribner's Sons, 1988.

McDermott, James. *Martin Frobisher: Elizabethan Privateer*. New Haven: Yale University Press, 2001.

McGhee, Robert. *The Arctic Voyages of Martin Frobisher*. Montreal: McGill-Queen's University Press, 2001.

McGoogan, Ken. *Ancient Mariner*. Toronto: HarperCollins Publishers Ltd., 2003.

_____. *Fatal Passage*. Toronto: HarperCollins Publishers Ltd., 2001.

Mowat, Farley. *Ordeal by Ice*. Toronto: McClelland and Stewart Ltd., 1960.

National Geographic Society. *National Geographic Expeditions Atlas*. Washington, DC: National Geographic Society, 2000.

Newman, Peter C. *Company of Adventurers*. Toronto: Penguin Books Canada Ltd., 1985.

Officer, Charles and Jake Page. *A Fabulous Kingdom*. New York: Oxford University Press, 2001.

Paine, Lincoln P. *Ships of Discovery and Exploration*. Boston: Houghton Mifflin Co., 2000.

Royal Canadian Mounted Police. *St. Roch: The Mounties' Arctic Schooner*. Vancouver: Pierway Inc., 2000.

Ruby, Robert. *Unknown Shore*. New York: Henry Holt and Co., 2001.

Ryan, Peter. *In Search of the Past: Explorers and Mapmakers*. London: Hamish Hamilton Children's Books, 1989.

Savours, Ann. *The Search for the North West Passage*. New York: St. Martin's Press, 1999.

Schuster, Carl. "Into the Great Bay," *The Beaver* 79, no. 4 (1999): 8–15.

Steele, Peter. *The Man Who Mapped the Arctic*. Vancouver: Raincoast Books, 2003.

Struzik, Edward. *Northwest Passage: The Quest for an Arctic Route to the East*. Toronto: Key Porter Books Limited, 1991.

Symons, Thomas H.B. *Meta Incognita: A Discourse of Discovery*. Hull, QC: Canadian Museum of Civilization, 1999.

Trevelyan, G.M. *History of England*. London: Longman Group UK Ltd., 1926.

Turner, Jack. *Spice: The History of A Temptation*. London: Harper Collins Publishers, 2004.

White, Howard, ed. *Raincoast Chronicles*. Madeira Park, BC: Harbour Publishing, 1983.

Wilkinson, Doug. *Arctic Fever*. Toronto: Clarke, Irwin & Co. Ltd., 1971.

Williams, Glyn. *Voyages of Delusion*. New Haven: Yale University Press, 2003.

Wilson, John. *John Franklin: Traveller on Undiscovered Seas*. Lantzville, BC: XYZ Publishing, 2001.

Wright, Rear Admiral S. Noel. *New Light on Franklin*. Ipswich, UK: W.S. Cowell Ltd., 1949.

Index

King William Island (King William Land), 92,
95, 96, 98, 99, 104, 108, 110, 111, 121, 136
Klengenberg, Christian, 116, 117, 120
Kodlunarn Island. *See* Countess of Warwick's
Island

Lancaster Sound, 53, 79, 83, 90, 106, 129
Larsen, Henry, 114–31, 132, 133, 137
lead line, 16, 44, 110, 119
Little Hall Island, 18, 22, 24
Lok, Michael, 16, 22–23, 27, 34

Mackenzie River, 65, 79, 91
Matonabbee, 56, 58–60, 61, 62, 63, 66
McClintock, Francis, 98–99
McClure, Robert, 97
Meta Incognita, 22
mining, 25, 27, 28, 31
Mistaken Straits. *See* Hudson Strait
Moose Factory, 85, 86
Muscovy Company, 15–16, 22, 38, 41, 44,
46, 135

north magnetic pole, 104, 108, 109–10
North Pole, 38, 40–41, 70, 104, 112–13
North West Company (NWC), 71–72, 84
Northwest Passage, 29, 34, 54, 59, 64, 69, 79,
82, 87, 93, 95, 97, 98, 101, 104, 110, 111,
114, 121, 122, 128, 129–30, 131, 132, 134,
136, 137
Norton, Moses, 56, 57, 58–59, 65
Nova Zembla, 37, 41, 42, 43, 44, 46, 47

Omdahl, Oscar, 116

Pasley, Corporal, 116–17, 118–19
Phillip II (of Spain), 12, 13, 35
piracy, 13, 35, 38
Point Turnagain, 74, 79
Portugal, 46, 55, 68, 135
Prickett, Abacuck, 49, 53
privateering, 13–14, 35

quadrant, 57, 59

Rae, John, 84–100, 111, 137
Richardson, Dr. John, 70, 75–76, 77, 78, 80,
84–85, 89, 90–91, 97

Royal Canadian Mounted Police (RCMP),
114–15, 116, 117, 118, 120, 121, 122, 125, 128,
129, 130, 131, 134, 137
Rupert Bay, 51

scurvy, 10, 33, 38–39, 51, 60, 75, 77, 86, 99, 100,
103, 112, 136
ships
Ayde, 23, 26, 27, 28, 29, 33
Dennys, 29, 31
Discovery, 49, 50, 52, 53
Erebus, 82, 83, 99, 127
Gabriel, 16, 17–18, 19, 20, 21, 23, 27, 32, 33
Gjøa, 104–105, 106–108, 110, 111, 112, 114,
123, 137
Half Moon, 46, 47–48
Hopewell, 38, 39, 40, 41, 42, 43, 44, 45
Judith, 29,
Michael, 16, 17, 23, 27, 29, 32, 33
St. Roch, 115, 118, 119–20, 121–22, 123–25,
126–27, 128, 130, 131, 137
Terror, 82, 83, 99, 127
Triumph, 35
Silk Road, 14
Simpson, Governor George, 87, 88, 89, 93
Spain, 12, 14, 15, 29, 35, 46, 55, 135
Spanish Armada, 35, 135
spices, 14, 38
Spitsbergen Islands, 39, 41, 54, 113

Ungava Bay, 50

Vancouver Maritime Museum, 131
Victoria Island, 92, 93, 117, 122

walrus, 40, 41, 43, 70
whaling, 41, 55, 114
William IV, 81, 82
Willoughby, Sir Hugh, 9–10, 41–42, 45, 135

yellow fever, 12
Yellowknife First Nation, 62, 72–73, 74, 75,
76, 78
York Factory, 71, 84, 88, 89, 90, 93

Acknowledgements

I would like to thank Susan Buss, the librarian at the Vancouver Maritime Museum, who helped me access books in the Henry Larsen Rare Book Room, and the very helpful staff at the Glenbow Museum Archives. I am also grateful for the services provided by the Calgary Public Library, the University of Calgary Library and the National Archives of Canada, as well as the Arctic Institute of North America and the National Maritime Museum in Greenwich, England.

Thanks are due to Ray Gilles for tipping me off about the exploits of his countryman, Sir Hugh Willoughby. Fellow writers Lisa Murphy-Lamb and Joan Dixon gave me valuable feedback, editor Lesley Reynolds helped me with improvements to this second edition, and my immediate family and friends were, as usual, encouraging and supportive. One final thank you must go to Bill Pitcher at Golden Photography for generously providing the author's photograph.

About the Author

Frances Hern enjoys sailing, but only where she is unlikely to encounter pirates, frostbite or scurvy. She also likes to have accurate charts and a Global Positioning System receiver on board so that her skipper knows where he is at all times.

This is Frances' second Amazing Story. Her first book, *Norman Bethune*, tells about the life of the Canadian doctor renowned worldwide for his surgical treatment of tuberculosis. As well as non-fiction, Frances writes poetry and children's fiction.